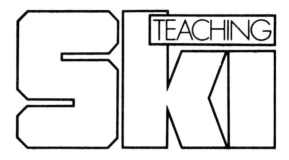

SKI TEACHING

John Shedden

FREDERICK MULLER LIMITED
LONDON

First published in Great Britain 1972 by
John Jones Cardiff Limited
This edition published 1980 by
Frederick Muller Limited, London NW2 6LE

British Library Cataloguing in Publication Data

Shedden, John
   Ski-teaching. – 2nd ed.
   1. Skis and skiing – Study and teaching
   I. Title
   796.9'3'07   GV854

ISBN 0–584–10477–4

Typeset by Computacomp (UK) Ltd, Fort William, Scotland, and
Printed in Great Britain by The Garden City Press Ltd, Herts

CONTENTS

FOREWORD

In my past career as a steeple-chase runner I was fortunate to have a coach, Geoffrey Dyson, who understood all of Isaac Newton's Laws of Motion. His teaching sessions were supported by demonstrations on frictionless platforms, with spinning weighted bicycle wheels, and slow-motion loop films of cats turning in the air to land on their feet. In essence, I was taught by a coach who fully comprehended body mechanics and therefore instructed me efficiently.

John Shedden, Director of Coaching for the English Ski Council, is in the Dyson mold of perceptive coaches. He has recognized that there is a right way of teaching skiing, and that it must be based on correct fundamental principles.

Mechanics, physiology and psychology are all essential components of ski teaching, and John Shedden, after many years of dedicated study, is the ideal person to make a rational and practical structure of these disciplines.

Unlike teaching in some other sport skills, 'stand-still' posturizing just does not work in ski instruction. Skiing is a dynamic exercise and once on the move either on snow or plastic, the performer can do things that are impossible when at rest. John Shedden's book *Ski Teaching* is a treatise about movement – that beautiful feeling of weightlessness that good ski technique produces. His teaching practices are designed to allow this feeling of release from gravity to be achieved more quickly and with less chagrin.

John Disley CBE
Sports Council
London SW 3

ACKNOWLEDGEMENTS

I would like to express my gratitude to those friends and colleagues who have helped me directly and indirectly with their advice, suggestions and moral support at various stages in the evolution of this book. These include Ian Thompson, Director of Physical Recreation at Stirling University; Robin Brock-Hollinshead, former National Coach, National Ski Federation of Great Britain; Roger Orgill, Regional Coach, Ski Council for Wales; Peter Lingard and the other members of staff of the Physical Education Department of Coventry College of Education; Ron James, Principal Lecturer in Environmental Studies, I. M. Marsh College of Education and Eric Rosenblatt, Chairman of the North West Ski Federation.

For their help in the experimental aspects of my work, and in the analysis of skiing skill, I would like to thank Karl Haas and Erich Moscher of the Austrian Professional Ski Teachers' Association; Georges Joubert, Director of the Ski School, University of Grenoble; Karl Fuchs, Colin Whiteside, Tony Rice and all the staff and pupils of the Austrian Ski School, Carrbridge, Scotland.

I would also like to acknowledge the help and inspiration given to me by the National Ski Federation of Great Britain, the British Association of Ski Instructors, Austrian Professional Ski Teachers' Association and the Professional Ski Instructors of America.

Finally my special thanks are due to Jeannine Spencer, Colin Whiteside, Karina Zarod, Jenny Dixon, Neil Shepperd and Sander Carling for their very patient help in the production of the photographs; to Mrs Valerie Siviter, Mrs Vivian Jennings and Mrs Beryl Wood for typing, and to Colin Le Good for reading, the original manuscripts.

J.S.

INTRODUCTION

It has been suggested that 90 per cent of children in schools learn to read in spite of their teachers, and in spite of the teaching methods employed.[1] It has further been suggested that the skill of the teacher could be measured by the success he achieves with the other 10 per cent. I have often wondered how true this is of skiing and ski-teaching.

Techniques, styles and teaching methods have been changing continually for over eighty years. Ski schools have evolved teaching systems which have been followed religiously by instructors and pupils alike, often in complete disregard of people's individual natures, temperaments and abilities. The pupils are told that what they learned last year (in the same school, perhaps even from the same instructor) is now out of date, and should be disregarded. This is clearly absurd, for people did learn to ski under the older systems and continue to do so under contemporary ones.

During the last twenty years, many changes in teaching methods have taken place. These changes have been influenced, in the first instance, by experiences of ski instructors in the field; secondly, by educational investigations which have been carried out as to how skilful performances can be developed, and, lastly, by the re-assessment of previously practised and accepted teaching methods and systems of instruction. By far the greater influence, however, has been the success of a particular ski racer or group of racers, and the techniques which he, or they, have used.

Ski-teaching systems have always been based upon the technique and styles of the best racers of the day. Ski instructors try to interpret these racers' movements, and teach them to beginners in the ski school.

In the past, the differences between racers and recreational skiers were not as great as they are today, and to some degree therefore, this approach to teaching beginners was justified.

Today, however, the average holiday skier is able to spend only a few weeks and weekends on the ski slopes, whereas the best racers of all the major skiing nations train for as much as ten months in the year. Today's racers benefit from intense scientific investigations, achieve better physical condition than ever before, and use specialized equipment. Their motivation is totally different from that of the recreational skier, and the new techniques which they develop are applicable at a level of competence seldom achieved by the majority of recreational skiers.

This does not mean that there should be separate techniques for competitors and recreational skiers, but rather that the wide variety of movements used by the racer should be introduced to the recreational skier at a level appropriate to his individual ability and needs.

There are no significant differences in the movements made by the top ski racers of all the major skiing nations, but there are many contradictions in the movements taught by the ski schools of these nations. This is mainly due to the fact that each nation has chosen different racers as its models and then stressed the importance of some of their movements and body positions to the neglect of others. The movements which were chosen to be built into the ski school system were often refined aspects of personal style, such as the extreme reverse shoulder of Stein Erikson, and not the fundamental movements governing balance, steering and adaptation to terrain.

Modern ski instruction should not ask students to imitate techniques which took the instructor anything up to ten years to learn, but should teach him those fundamental movements which will enable him to develop his skiing skill at a rate appropriate to his own personal capabilities and desires.

This book has been written for all skiers who are interested in, or concerned with, ski teaching. The need for such a book was first realised when, as a trainer and examiner for the British Association of Ski Instructors, I was asked by candidates to recommend reading material which would furnish them with information relevant to the courses. The same request in relation to courses within the National coaching scheme has determined the bias of the text.

The aim of this book will be achieved if it enables skiers to understand a little more about what it is they are trying to learn; and if it encourages ski instructors to take a fresh look at their aims, and methods of achieving them.

In the past we have been concerned with trying to teach specific 'school form' techniques to 'average' skiers, rather than teaching individuals how to control themselves while sliding down a mountainside. In the future we must think less about teaching styles and techniques and think more about teaching people.

As I revise this second edition of *Ski Teaching* seven years after the original edition was written, I reflect with pleasure how Ski Instruction has, universally, moved onto a common, but broad base and, in doing so, begun to recognize the needs of the individuals who are doing the learning.

A specific area of satisfaction has been the growth of individual coaching available to skiers in the home nations of Great Britain and the development of training schemes which are providing skiers with opportunities to pursue their sport in their own ways. Advanced recreational skiing courses, Junior and Senior racing and Freestyle coaching are now available to all who are keen to develop personal excellence.

Readers will be interested to note that some of the skiers used to illustrate this second edition of *Ski Teaching* were introduced to skiing on artificial slopes and have risen to international competition since the first edition of *Ski Teaching* seven years ago.

I have resisted the temptation to extend this book to cover these aspects of advanced skiing, retaining my premise that a sound ground-schooling is the best possible base for those with 'great expectations'.

[1] *The Slow Reader* R. C. Ablewhite, Heinemann 1967.

CHAPTER ONE

A Universal System of Ski Instruction

A pair of skis found in a peat bog, near Hoting in Sweden, indicates that men have been skiing for nearly 4,500 years. It was not until 1866, near Christiania (now Oslo) that the first skiing competition was held. It took nearly 4,400 years for the Scandinavians to develop skiing into a sport. It was left to Norwegian students and Englishmen to introduce the sport of skiing in the Alps in any forceful way.

In 1890, Fridtjof Nansen wrote an account of how he crossed Greenland on skis in 1888. This book, the first to be written about skiing, inspired mountain men throughout the world, and in 1896 an Austrian, Mathias Zdarsky, wrote the first methodical analysis of Alpine ski

1. *Austrian skiers circa 1900*

technique. His book, *Lilienfelder Skilauf Technik*, was based upon movements which he himself invented while adapting Nansen's descriptions of Nordic techniques to Alpine conditions. Zdarsky had never seen another skier prior to 1896.

Zdarsky in turn laid the foundations for further work in the field of ski technique. W. R. Rickmers, one of Zdarsky's principal disciples, wrote,

> To him (Zdarsky) we owe a published theory of skiing as specially applicable to steep and difficult Alpine ground; while many, including the writer, enjoy the honour of being his disciples. This honour was not, in the first instance, without its drawbacks, for a theory, especially if it be new and original, is a fertile source of dissension.

(page 15, *Ski Running*. Published by Horace Cox, London, 1905. The first book about skiing in the English language.)

Even in 1905, then, ski technicians were not without their controversies. Unknown to Zdarsky, skiing was developing in Switzerland and Germany, after a crossing of the Bernese Oberland on ski, by Dr Paulcke. The centre of this development was in the Black Forest, though it quickly spread to Freiburg, where the university students were energetic in their support of the new sport.

W. Rickmers continues:

> The differences between the Zdarsky school and the Black Forest school threatened to assume alarming proportions for, strange to say, both sides had seen little of each other, and a host of misunderstandings arose between them over theoretical opinions concerning style and fastening.

Differences in opinions of how skiing should be taught still exist in 1979.

Between 1905 and 1970 many books were written on ski technique and teaching methods. The most influential include *Der Alpine Skilauf* by Colonel Bilgeri, and the classic of its day *How to Ski*, to be followed by *Skiing Turns*, both by Vivian Caulfield. These books were the first to analyse the dynamics of skiing, and there are few movements used in recreational skiing today which Vivian Caulfield did not describe most accurately in his books.

These were followed by *Der Wunder des Schnee Schuhs* by Hannes Schneider and Arnold Fank and *The History of Skiing* by Arnold Lunn, who introduced to the world what we now know as slalom racing.

In 1936, Giovanni Testa and Dr Eugene Matthias wrote *Naturliches Schilaufen*. Emile Allais's book *Ski Français* followed, leading the world into the 1940s. National ski schools were now emerging and in the early 1950s Austria took the lead from France with Stefan Kurckenhauser's *New Official Austrian Ski System*. The most recent publication to have a powerful effect on ski teaching was G. Joubot and J. Vuarnet's book, *How to Ski the New French Way*, published in English by Kaye and Ward, London, in 1967.

As W. Rickmers has observed, lack of communication was the greatest cause of controversies in ski technique in 1905, and this was still true in 1950.

In 1951, Dr Kruckenhauser invited national ski schools to send delegations to a conference at Zurs in Austria. This was the first ever international ski school congress, and out of it Interski was formed. This organization was founded to increase international communication and to exchange ideas concerning ski instruction with the eventual aim of unifying the world's various ski instructional systems. Interski congresses are now held every four years, and serve as showplaces for each nation's instructional ideas and technical innovations.

During the 1960s many of these ideas were 'borrowed' by other nations and a semblance of uniformity began to emerge. However in 1968, at the eighth Interski Congress, in Aspen, Colorado, USA, a significant step was made towards total unification. Karl Gamma, Director of the Swiss Ski Schools, presented a paper which proposed a three-tier ski school system. This system would bring about the unification of ski teaching methods for beginners, but allow for national differences at a higher, competitive level.

The reasoning behind Herr Gamma's system, and his own belief in its practicability, was based upon recognition of the many basic elements of technique used both by young children learning to ski and the world's top racers, irrespective of their nationality and that nation's particular ski instruction system. He also reasoned that most recreational skiers do not want to win gold medals at the Olympic Games, they simply want to learn to ski. They want to learn how to ski efficiently on different types of terrain and every kind of snow. For this they require basic techniques.

If the skier really masters these, his goals have been achieved. Only a few skiers are in the most advanced classes, and the ability of the best ski school pupils seldom improves beyond the level of the instruction they have received. The specialists are trained in teams and clubs.

(Karl Gamma, page 89, *Congress Report, 8 Interski, Aspen*. Published by Interski Inc., Denver, USA, 1968.)

He further argued that if ski schools failed to recognize that the recreational skier required training relevant to his needs, then agreement would never be reached on standard approaches to elementary instruction because of the influence of the competitive image. He asked that the members of the Congress, the ski schools, should clarify to themselves and to their public the exact nature of their activities. He suggested that this could be done by dividing the whole field of ski instruction into three

areas, which would form the three tiers of the national ski schools.
    Karl Gamma's proposals:

Division of Levels in Ski Instruction
1. The Ground School. Instruction in basic techniques.
2. The High School. Improving and extending skiing skills.
3. Racing School. National racing and training scheme.

The Ground School
The aim of this part of the ski schools is to teach basic parallel skiing. It is in this section of the ski school that the need for international uniformity is greatest because they provide the elementary technical training for the majority of skiers. People travelling abroad from such countries as Britain and France for winter skiing holidays enjoy visiting different countries each year; and skiers from countries with natural ski slopes like to test their skills on foreign slopes. But, at present, the enjoyment of this change of skiing venue is often marred more by differences in the teaching methods employed in different countries than by the problems posed by the different languages. Now is the time to eradicate the out-dated idea that international ski racing success depends on the content and quality of a 'national' ski technique and instructional method.

    In Alpine countries, a racer who reaches the notice of the general public has undoubtedly had at least ten or twelve years' experience, and it is unlikely that many of these were spent in a ski school.

    The racers set the pace and provide the inspiration for all lesser mortals. They stand in the harsh limelight to represent their countries – these are the most active and influential people in skiing. This is as it should be; but how relevant are their activities to the original intent of the holiday-maker and recreational skier? At present, ski schools promote a national image in addition to teaching students to ski. 'Ski schools should serve skiing and tourism in a more passive way.' (Page 91, *Karl Gamma*.)

    The most important person should be the student, and a unified, international teaching system would enable the ski school to concentrate on instructing its students and not on enhancing its own image and reputation in the eyes of other nations.

    It would be naive to think that ski schools were organizations with altruistic motives for teaching pupils to ski. They are commercial organizations run by hard-headed businessmen and, while it is true that they depend on a certain level of customer satisfaction for their profits, it cannot be denied that a major part of their business is with novice skiers. Only a true cynic would argue that ski schools introduce new and sometimes contradictory techniques in order to inhibit pupils' progress, so that they may remain within the ski school for longer than may be ideally necessary, but it is certain that most commercial organizations see the need for the introduction of a 'new product' at regular intervals if they are going to hold or increase their share of the market.

It is a sad but significant fact that the 'drop out' rate among novice skiers is put at between 65 per cent and 85 per cent.

The differences between recreational and competitive skiers must still be recognized. The ground school can lay the foundations for both, though it is more likely that future racers will emerge from schools, ski clubs and other, non-commercial organizations, than from the commercial ski school.

Moreover, an internationally agreed ground school of ski instruction would enable ski schools to concentrate on other important matters, such as improved teaching methods, better training for ski instructors, investigation of the psychological aspects of learning, language and communication problems and other issues concerned with safety and accident avoidance.

The High School
This section of the ski schools would be concerned with refining the basic techniques learned in the ground school. It is here that overall skiing skill would be developed, applying the basic techniques to as wide a variety of environmental conditions as possible. International rivalry between ski schools of different countries should continue to function at this level.

This level of the ski school could serve as a 'filter' between the ground school and the racing school. The beginner would be shielded from advanced racing techniques which he would find confusing or difficult, and also from those which are of only temporary interest, i.e. the fashions which come and go depending on who wins the medals and what peculiarities of personal style he may have.

This level of the school would strive to interpret the actions of the successful racers and the most advanced recreational skiers into meaningful techniques which could be learned by anyone who has the basic abilities and the necessary motivation.

The ski teacher at this level must be selected from the élite. 'At this level explanation becomes a problem and demonstration becomes an art.' (Page 93, *Karl Gamma.*)

The Racing School
In the racing school, it would be possible to build on the broad foundations laid by the first and second parts of the ski school. Strength, conditioning and motivation would become as important as techniques.

Tactics would be studied and the aims of the students would be clearly defined. The racing school should lead to a separation of the racers from the purely recreational skiers. The ski teacher becomes a trainer.

To be successful, the trainer should have gained considerable racing experience himself, and would combine this with his technical expertise to teach students, young and old, to ski to the best of their ability. Above all, he must complement these abilities with an extensive knowledge of ski mechanics, dynamics, human psychology and physiology, as these are the most important at this level.

It is from this level of the ski schools that recreational holiday skiers would receive very specialist training, in freestyle skiing as well as racing, if they so wished. Competition and international rivalry would ensure that adjustments to techniques and methods would continue to be made, and so our knowledge of skiing would always be increasing and improving.

We can profit most from the knowledge gained during intense competition, but it must be used in a constructive and logical way, and it should be applied only at the levels of learning where it will be most beneficial.

Herr Gamma's proposals of the three tier structure for commercial ski schools had considerable impact upon the members of the Congress. His views were recognized as being honest, perceptive and relevant to the problems of today. Considerable sympathy for his views were expressed by many delegates and a desire was expressed to investigate his proposals in the immediate future.

If milestones are made at Interski, this congress must go down in history as one of the most significant. It brought together nearly 1,000 of the world's best instructors and teachers, whose purpose was to learn, compare and perform. Past differences, past grievances and misunderstandings were thrown aside in the interest of skiing and ski technique.
(Willy Schaefler, President of Interski, Aspen, 27 April 1968.)

Professor Kruckenhauser, now the lifetime honorary president of Interski, predicted that 'from this congress there will be new understandings and progress'.

The next major step forward occurred very soon after the Aspen Interski conference. In September of the same year, the Swiss Ski Instructors' Association invited the professional Ski Instructors' Associations of each nation to send a small delegation to Zermatt.

A conference was held at the Hotel Christiania, an apt choice considering the nature of the subject under discussion. Practical sessions took place high on the Theodule glacier, often beginning as early as seven a.m., to take advantage of the late summer snow conditions.

The British Association of Ski Instructors sent three delegates: Ken Dickson from Aviemore, as demonstrator of the British system as it was then; Frith Finlayson, secretary of the Association, and myself, whose duties included translating and recording on film the theoretical and practical activities of the conference.

The purpose of the conference was for the members to discuss the practicability of accepting Karl Gamma's proposals, particularly with regard to the ground school.

Delegates were asked to demonstrate their own particular approaches to teaching up to and including basic parallel turns. Differences were observed, and discussed at great length – often into the early hours. A reasonable level of agreement was reached after the major points of disagreement had been clarified by discussion and explanation.

The conference ended with a feeling of hope for the future. A determination by most members to work towards unity in the basic techniques was evident and, since the smallness of the number of delegates permitted greater understanding of individual problems, such unity might soon be achieved.

Britain has a relatively small instructional network, and the British Association of Ski Instructors has already gone a long way towards bringing techniques and methods into line with the general trend in Europe.

Modern educational thinking has had considerable effect upon this trend, and the ski instructional systems of Europe are moving slowly away from the rigid final forms of the 50s and 60s and encouraging a freer, more individual approach to learning to ski. Such an approach requires a more flexible teaching method than has been evident before, using techniques which allow each individual to benefit fully from class, as opposed to individual tuition. The wide stance (that is, skiing with feet hip width apart) and the *Grundschwung* or basic swing turn (where the student learns to steer towards and skid away from the fall line in an elementary fashion) are the two major innovations which the world has grown to accept since the 1968 Interski. This acceptance is due in no small part to the very widespread influence of M. Georges Joubert's and Jean Vuarnet's book, *How to Ski the New French Way*, and the adoption of these techniques by the Austrian Ski School.

However, things were not progressing quite so smoothly as Herr Gamma might have wished.

Interski was reconvened at Garmisch-Partenkirchen, Germany, in January 1971. The theme was to be *Einheit uber alles* – Unity above all. Or so the majority of the delegates thought. Professor Kruckenhauser appeared to think otherwise. His presentation of the '*Wellen* Technique' hit the congress like a bombshell. The technique itself was not new; everyone already knew it through *avalement*. M. Joubert had presented it more than adequately in his book in 1967, and each nation already had elements of it in its advanced classes. But the Professor was now proposing that students be introduced to it as a much earlier stage. Or was he?

Heinz Nobauer wrote in the Fischer Ski Company magazine *Ski Welt*, 'Austria is again the leader in the development of technique'.[1] Karl Gamma was quoted as saying, 'We feel manipulated and stabbed in the back by the Austrians'.[2]

Even Heinz Nobauer supported this view, writing as he did, 'The "*Wellen* Technique" has torpedoed the natural unification of ski teaching'.[3]

However, perhaps the feelings of skiers generally were expressed by Sepp Ender of Lichtenstein when he said,

> Every nation at this congress has done its best to make propaganda for its own country. Beginners all over the world need a clear line for instruction. How can they take lessons in your country and then mine if there is no basic system? If this congress does not develop this, and it hasn't, then it is a fraud.[4]

After the major comments had been voiced, the Professor attempted to justify his country's demonstrations and restore some sense of unification. 'We were misunderstood,' he said. 'We were trying to indicate how ski instruction could develop. Our main point was to show how strongly the "*Wellen*" movements will influence teaching, all the way to the basics'.[5] He also gave full credit to M. Joubert for his brilliant work on *avalement*, and predicted the abandoning of final forms by the Austrians in their teaching system. The influence of the *wellen* or *avalement* techniques can be seen very clearly in the Austrian Professional Ski Teachers' publication *Schilehrplan* (Ski Teachers' Handbook), published in January 1972. This book stresses the use of the wide stance, the basic swing turn and other techniques which are now universally accepted.

One disappointing aspect of the Interski congresses has been, however, that so much time has been spent on deciding *what* to teach, that very little time has been devoted to *how* to teach. Such questions as *how* do skiers learn? Why do people learn in different ways and at different rates? What kinds of physical types learn which manoeuvres most easily? How much strength is required to learn skiing as opposed to simply skiing? Which skills, perceptual and motor, need to be learned? These and many other questions remain unanswered.

The question 'how?' has not altogether been ignored, however. At Garmisch, the French and the Austrians both gave their demonstrations on shorter than usual skis: approx. 175 cm long. Learning to ski on short skis has been advocated for quite a long time now, but there are many dyed-in-the-wool traditionalists who cannot see the advantages of such an approach, even though the major skiing brains of the world now believe that learning on short skis must be beneficial. The general skiing public still has reservations.

Short skis as an aid to learning were introduced to the second Interski congress at Davos, Switzerland, in 1952.

Karl Koller, director of the ski school in Kitzbuhel, gave a demonstration and a lecture, enumerating the advantages of using short skis for learning. At this time many skiers found Herr Koller's ideas amusing and many more found them unacceptable. They claimed it degraded skiing. Really, unless skis reached the palm of the hand when above the head, they could not really be considered as skis, they said. This view, extreme as it is, has been held and still is held to a lesser degree by many people, who, in Karl Koller's words, 'would not want to be seen on these toothpicks, which immediately expose them as beginners'.

The values of Karl Koller's ideas could not be denied by serious instructors who were truly concerned with the learning problems of beginners.

An important variation of the short ski aid to learning began in 1959 when an American, Cliff Taylor, began experimenting with short skis.

During the mid 1960s Cliff Taylor's 'Graduated Length' method of learning (GLM for short) appeared. This method involves learning basic skiing movements with a wide stance posture, initially on very short skis, usually 3 feet long. Within three or four periods of instruction the student repeats his efforts and develops them on longer skis, usually 5 feet long. When rhythmical, linked, basic swing turns can be made down the fall line, the student is considered to be ready to use regular-length skis. Cliff Taylor has shown that this can be expected to occur after the fifth period of instruction, or after about 10 hours' skiing practice.

These new ideas were slow in crossing the Atlantic and the Alps but in the late 1960s M. Robert Blanc, who was denied any prior knowledge of Taylor's work, introduced to France very similar, some would say identical, ideas through his book *Skier en 3 joures* (1970) with Pierre Gruneberg.

M. Blanc's ideas have gained considerable ground in up to 35 per cent of all French ski schools and can be seen in action at first hand, in his *ski evolutif* classes at Les Arc.

The American journal *Ski* (vol. 35 no. 4, 1970) conducted a comparative test between the GLM, the new Austrian and the contemporary American systems of teaching. The findings indicated that the total time required to learn to ski at speed using basic parallel turns was approximately the same for each method, but the GLM and Austrian methods reached higher skiing speeds sooner. An increase in safe skiing speed in each system was coincidental with the introduction into that system of a side skid phase to the turns (this is facilitated by shorter skis).

The results of these and many other tests carried out by Karl Koller,

Martin Puchtler in Germany, and myself at Karl Fuch's ski school in Scotland, between 1966 and 1970, indicate quite clearly that shorter skis will enable beginners to learn the basic movements of skiing more easily than longer skis, and pupils will therefore be able to use lifts and ski on a wider variety of terrain earlier than they would normally be able to.

A drawback of the GLM method is the increased capital expenditure required to equip the ski school/hire with two or three pairs of skis per person. From a practical point of view, the system now adopted by the Austrian ski schools and the British Association of Ski Instructors, of using one length of ski for all beginners, seems to the one most likely to be accepted generally.

The length recommended is 170 cm, though consideration would be taken of very small light persons, and a second length of 150 cm will possibly become available for such persons. Using the one length of ski, the student will learn to ski on all terrain, and will change to longer skis only if and when he needs to for reasons of stability in racing, etc.

The short skis will also enable older people to continue to enjoy their skiing, at a time when they might otherwise give up because they lack the strength needed to control longer skis. The attendant risks will also be greatly reduced, a factor of considerable psychological importance at all stages of learning, but especially as the student advances in years.

Commercial interests and the endless search for knowledge will ensure that ski techniques and ski teaching systems will continue to change. The struggle to establish a universal system of ski instruction will be a hard one, and allowances must always be made for innovations and original ideas which will make skiing easier to learn for a larger number of people.

The Interski congresses have shown that unity is possible: it only requires that those responsible for determining national policies can differentiate between the basic, universal requirements of beginners, and the transient fashions and fads of more advanced skiers. The three tier system proposed by Karl Gamma would go a long way towards securing this.

The universal acceptance of a ground school in skiing is of particular relevance to artificial slope ski instructors in Great Britain.

For ski instructors on the snow, it is very easy to slip subtly from the basic techniques of the ground school to the application of these techniques in the higher school; indeed, it is often impossible to separate the two as skiers become more mobile at the top end of the school and begin to use a wide variety of terrain to reinforce their learning. The artificial ski slope is a relatively constant environment restricted in shape, angle and texture, and the opportunities for developing basic techniques into the realm of the high school are relatively few.

The essential use of such ski slopes must therefore be as a medium on which the basic techniques of the ground school can be learned and practised. In fact, the artificial ski slope could possibly be more suitable than snow for this in relation to certain aspects of learning to ski. This will be discussed further in Chapter Five.

Techniques which may be more applicable to the high school and even the racing school than to the ground school can, of course, be practised on artificial ski slopes, but only in isolation. They cannot be practised in precisely the same context as they would be used when on the snow.

The role of the artificial ski slope instructor is therefore to instruct students in the basic techniques of the ground school, with the added possibility on large slopes of coaching more advanced skiers in particular aspects of technique which can be practised out of the environmental context that they would normally be performed in.

The artificial ski slope instructor should be more flexible than his snow counterpart, in as much as he will be preparing students to ski in all parts of Europe, on a wide variety of terrain, and possibly under different ski teaching systems.

Frith Finlayson, Director of Training for the British Association of Ski Instructors, reinforced this view in his summary of training address to the NSFGB senior coaches' conference at Plas y Brennin on 19 October 1971, when he said, 'The teaching on artificial ski slopes has to be of a higher standard than that on snow'.

Bearing this in mind, the artificial ski slope instructor can take his aims today from those of the ground schools of tomorrow. These must be to teach students how to control themselves and their equipment in a wide variety of sliding situations, and to teach the fundamental motor and perceptual skills of skiing which can be applied, under further instruction, in a wide variety of ways depending on the students' abilities, attitudes and desires, in relation to the prevailing terrain.

Strebske Pleso, Czechoslovakia, reconvened the 10th Interski Congress in January 1975. The seeds of revolution were set and watered at this meeting when Erhard Gatterman and Dr Walter Küchler presented West Germany's paper entitled: 'Today's skiing — universal, functional and student orientated'. While crediting Austrian 'leg play' technique, and Italian 'anticipation' as strong influences on their technical thinking, they made the powerful point that 'The time of the marked national ski schools — meaning national ski technique — is over'.

Dr Küchler went on to say that 'the technique of a good skier is not based on one single denominator any more. One can use very different techniques according to the aids (of the pupils) and to the situation.' He then made what was considered to be a strong attack on Austria by stating that 'the principle of the *Red Thread* of continuity is dead'.

The demonstration by the Federal Republic of Germany subsequently included pupils as well as Instructors, showing how different ages, builds and aims can influence a learning programme.

The Professional Ski Instructors of America reinforced Germany's approach by considering skiing as an activity in which skilful performances could develop.

This introduced many considerations beyond the purely technical ones of the then current technique dogmas.

As a result of the obvious visual impact of the precise formation skiing which is the focus of Interski's activities on the slopes, too many delegates failed to realize the significance of Germany's and America's presentations, dismissing them as 'cranks' and 'intellectuals'. Nevertheless, their influence was the most far reaching in the following years. Even Austria is now talking of 'form and situation skiing' – a small concession to the difference between pure and applied technique.

An apparent rebel in the Austrian camp, Karl Koller, who had for so long advocated short skis, presented, through Professor Kruckenhauser, an inspiring programme of children learning in a specially built 'terrain garden' (see illustration 2). This idea, in which the specific terrain forms

2. *Hans Kuwall demonstrates 'terrain garden' at Interski*

virtually cause the skier to adopt certain postures and perform basic techniques, has subsequently been developed by many teachers and its application to adult learning was to be shown by Germany at the next Interski Congress.

Strebske Pleso also saw the introduction of Ballet and Aerial, i.e.

Freestyle, skiing by Germany, America and Canada as part of their programmes aimed at pupils' requirements and interests.

3.   *Freestyle skiing, developed in America and introduced to Interski in 1975, offers self-expression and a challenge to advanced skiers*

On the 'pure technique' front, modern equipment – refined skis and binding, comfortable highly supportive boots – was helping to realize one of Karl Gamma's aims, the unifying of basic demonstration forms.

Great emphasis on quiet postures and accurate technique with exaggerated movements removed was evident. The Austrians had moved from their earlier low crouch to a 'middle' position, the Canadians hardly appeared to unweight at all and the French had reduced their 'projection circular' so much that, when everyone changed sweaters at the end of the Congress, differentiation on a 'national' basis was all but impossible.

The next four years between congresses saw the quiet development of teaching theory applied to skiing.

This has been hastened, in many cases, by the influences being brought to bear through the emergent 'non-professional ski instructor' organizations. These represent the interests of club and educational skiing, often through 'coaching schemes' which are concerned with the promotion of excellence in sportive skiers, rather than the leisure and purely recreational holiday skiing with which ski schools are concerned.

The Eleventh Interski Congress reconvened in January 1979 in Zao, Yamagata prefecture, Japan. The opening lecture on Alpine Skiing from

Sweden, stressed the need for an imaginative approach to solving pupils problems and was illustrated by the 'use of teaching aids (slalom poles) at all levels'.

Professor Hopichler followed for Austria, conceding the need for pupil consideration but confining this to the first paragraph of his stimulating lecture which considered the varied possibilities for turn initiation, entitled 'Step Turns or Parallel; What; When; How?'

> In ski instruction the 'either or' is being replaced with 'as well – as well'. Mono-thinking and thread of continuity do not meet anymore the manifold teaching and skiing situations. But too extended technical and, even more, a methodological variety, hinders a simple way which is necessary for mass instruction. The liberty to be able to consider a situation gives way to the responsibility to have it considered properly.

But the issue was not to rest there.

Horst Abraham presented a stunning lecture, despite a breakdown in Japanese visual aid equipment, improvising and joking his way through what was perhaps the most far reaching paper presented at an Interski Congress.

His lecture, notably prepared by members of his PSIA (Professional Ski Instruction of America) Educational Committee, was a clear indictment of previous doctrines but pointed also to future possibilities and, in particular, the emergence of coaching as a valid activity at all levels and not merely at the highest levels of competition.

> Reflecting on past Interski events it becomes apparent that contributions were made almost exclusively in the field of ski technique. Methodological matters have gotten little attention, although we are deeply indebted to Karl Koller and his 'childrens' terrain garden' concept.
>
> At the last Congress, our contribution, 'skills and skills development', was viewed with raised eyebrows – we did not believe the time was ripe for you to look at our proposals seriously.
>
> We believe that this year's contribution may fall upon different soil.

And, indeed, it did, although there was still a great deal of stony ground, some sadly within the British delegation. Mr Abraham's references to psychological research, to communication theory and then to the basic skills (as opposed to techniques) of skiing provided the cornerstones of discussion which dominated the remainder of the Congress.

It was very rewarding to hear such reinforcement of the concepts presented in Chapter Four of *Ski Teaching* despite the eight years and eleven thousand mile distance between them.

The Federal Republic of Germany reinforced the argument for greater consideration of teaching methods, and Switzerland's contribution, through Karl Gamma, made a plea for coordination of teaching terminology. Great Britain's lecture, presented with great presence and humour by John Hyndes, considered the effects that terrain, both artificial and narrow corries, had in determining the use of technique in Great Britain and most specifically the 'Direct Method' of learning parallel skiing.

The final presentations were given by our magnificent hosts the Japanese, who managed to present a blend of modern thinking. Their 'Austrian connection' goes back to the end of the last century and their imitative ability, evident in all the ski school classes in Zao, ensured that their team looked almost more Austrian than the Austrians. Their message stressed the need for greater consideration of the pupils' needs and a break from the rigid doctrines of the past.

Of special interest to me was their presentation of an aid to learning through perceptual acuity. It is perhaps a sign of the times that I had to travel half way around the world to see a demonstration of 'lines on the slope', to indicate 'where' to turn – a method introduced by the Author

4. *Interski 1979. Japanese demonstrate aids in development of perceptual abilities*

and used with great success on many artificial ski slopes in England (see Chapter Five) – given by the Japanese (see illustration 4).

The stark contrast between the dogma of national, 'commercial' ski schools and the more open, non-professional ski instructors' organizations was illustrated within the seminar sessions of the latter when Professor Hans Zehetmayer of Austria excused the confusion caused by Franz Hopichler's lecture, but reinforced his concepts, combining them with Horst Abraham's acclaimed arguments for a 'skills' approach. He admitted that this increased the complexity of knowledge and abilities required by ski instructors but was confident that such a step was both necessary and possible.

> This means an additional burden for the students of ski instruction because the theoretical and practical things to learn have become more numerous. Just like the good skier who can adjust himself to different situations because of his diversity in movements, the good instructor should be able to adapt himself to the different types of pupils with the help of a greater variety of teaching methods.
>
> (Prof Hans Zehetmayer, Secretary of International
> Non-Professional Ski Instructors' Association.)

In order to be able to dispense his responsibility fully, therefore, the ski instructor should add to his knowledge of skiing an awareness of some of the important psychological factors which affect the acquisition of skill in general and skiing skill in particular. In addition, the artificial ski slope instructor should have a basic knowledge of pre-ski training in order that he can help his students to increase their physical fitness either prior to, or during, training.

From an historical point of view, it has been Great Britain, more than any other country, that has concentrated on pre-ski instruction. This is, no doubt, due to the immense enthusiasm of British skiers in spite of their lack of opportunities to practise skiing in a practical situation.

The Ski Club of Great Britain, and the Central Council of Physical Recreation, have a long tradition of conducting pre-ski classes. These were often held in conjunction with Local Education Authorities.

The concept of pre-ski training has changed during the past decade. It is no longer believed that there is any transfer of training from learning to 'snowplough' in a gymnasium to snowploughing under gravity on a snow slope. One can only learn to perform skiing techniques while actually sliding downhill under the influence of gravity.

The emphasis has, therefore, moved from learning static skiing positions, to moving around on skis in non-sliding situations in order to learn how to cope with their size and weight. The most valuable aspect of pre-ski training, however, is its effect upon an individual's physical fitness.

Chapter Two provides an up-to-date approach to pre-ski training which can be adopted by the reader wishing to increase his fitness for skiing. It is also intended to provide a guide for ski instructors who incorporate pre-ski training into their schemes of work. The approach which is recommended is applicable at all levels of skiing ability, from the absolute beginner to the aspiring Olympic racer.

Pre-ski training does not form any part of the curriculum in the ground school as conceived by Karl Gamma. It is unlikely that commercial ski schools anywhere will ever include pre-ski training in their systems, except for those aspects which deal with equipment familiarization and 'walking on the flat', during the initial stages of learning.

Though pre-ski training has no internationally recognized place in the proposed ground school, its importance to British skiing remains, at least until every skier has the opportunity to use a plastic ski slope to practise on whenever he wants to. For this reason, pre-ski training has not been included in Chapter Four, which is concerned with the fundamentals of skiing that are relevant to the aims of the ground school of ski instruction.

CHAPTER TWO

Pre-Ski Training

In modern society, the average man and woman spend most of their time either sitting down or sleeping. Their bodies get very little exercise during the day's work. We nearly all sit in buses, trains or cars when going to work, sit in offices or stand at benches when at work, and then sit in front of a television set or a cinema screen in the evenings.

To function at their full physical potential, our bodies need exercise, and since most of us do not get enough exercise in the course of our work, we must seek other ways of working our bodies to keep them healthy. Some people do take part in a wide variety of activities which tend to work their bodies at a satisfactory level. Many more, however, do very little in the way of physical exercise either through lack of time, facilities or opportunity. Such people may find that they cannot do justice to themselves when they take a skiing holiday; their lack of physical fitness prevents them from enjoying their skiing to the full. The low level of skill of the beginner will mean that he will be subjected to considerable physical effort, which will further reduce his enjoyment unless he prepares himself beforehand.

Pre-ski training provides the means for skiers to prepare themselves physically, and to some extent, mentally, for their chosen sport.

Pre-ski training can be carried out in a class under instruction, in small groups of like-minded friends or at home alone. The value of the training will increase in relation to the frequency of the training sessions. One per day is not too much while one per week should be considered as a minimum.

In recent years, the enthusiastic desire to learn to ski before going to the snow has caused many pre-ski classes to be run, where the aim has been to teach students how to ski, as well as to improve their fitness. Students have been shown many 'skiing positions' and have even gone through the motions of 'making' ski turns. My observations and experiments during five autumns of pre-ski instructing, and fifteen winters as a ski school manager, chief instructor and coach have indicated that there is no positive correlation between what is learned in such pre-ski classes and what is required on the snow in order to control the skis. It is extremely unlikely that anyone can learn to ski without actually sliding downhill under the influence of gravity.

The increase in the numbers of artificial ski slopes, combined with the most modern methods of ski teaching, has meant that pre-ski training can now concentrate on preparing the skier physically for his skiing.

This preparation can include the student's accommodation of his equipment. A pre-ski class which has access to skis and boots can provide an ideal opportunity for the student to learn how to cope with this equipment. The problems that very long, heavy 'feet' can cause can be overcome in comfort and without using too much valuable skiing time. The student who prepares himself in this way will find that he can control himself adequately when he arrives at the snow. Without feeling too clumsy with or restricted by his equipment, he will be able to set about learning to ski downhill straight away.

Pre-Ski Exercises

Pre-ski training can consist of everyday activities as well as specially conceived exercises. All pre-ski training activities can be considered in four distinct groupings. For convenience, I have listed these groupings below and numbered them One to Four. When you are preparing a training schedule either for yourself or for a group of skiers in a 'pre-ski class', select exercises from each group to ensure a balanced course.

Exercises from *Group Four* will only be possible if you have access to equipment. Exercises from the other three groups have been designed for use without special equipment. Suitable clothing should be worn for all exercises.

Exercise Groups

Group One   – non-specialized, warming-up and general fitness exercises.

Group Two   – specific strength and fitness exercises.

Group Three   – flexibility and mobility exercises.

Group Four   – equipment familiarization exercises.

The exercises listed here are only a small number of the many possible ones. They are well tried and will prove more than adequate for all recreational skiers, and are used to advantage by competitive skiers also.

Group One

These are non-specialized exercises which can be used for general fitness training in everyday situations, or for warming up prior to a circuit training session, or indeed a period of skiing on the snow. There are distinct advantages in having warm muscles prior to starting your exercise sessions or your day's skiing.

(a)   Warm muscles work more efficiently than cold ones, as extra oxygen and glucose are available due to an increase in the circulation rate. This offsets fatigue.

(b)   The antagonist muscles are less likely to be injured if they are warm. (These are the muscles which have to lengthen on one side of a joint to enable the muscles on the other side of the joint to produce power by contracting.)

(c)   Warm muscles increase their rate of contraction and can, therefore, produce more power per contraction. In addition, their relaxation rate is increased even more, thereby increasing the capacity of the muscles to work.

Exercises for Group One

1. *Walk upstairs* instead of using lifts, etc. Similarly, walk instead of ride whenever possible.
2. *Cycling.* Distance or sprint.
3. *Jogging.* Up and downhill over uneven ground. Be sure to wear boots or strong shoes. Tighten the laces and avoid shoes that are too large.

5.   *Shan Usher, junior skier, running through slalom course set on grass*

Avoid wet terrain – a slip could be dangerous. Use a light, bouncing step and do not run out of control. Competitive skiers can mix jogging and running with slalom training. Running through courses set on the beach or on grass. Course reading ability will be improved in addition to cardio-respiratory efficiency (see illustration 5).

4. *Running on the pavement.* Pay special attention to avoid stepping on the cracks or joints of the paving stones.
5. *Running on the spot.* Lift the knees high.
6. *Skipping with a rope.* High knee-raising.
7. *Jumping.* Both feet simultaneously. Lift knees as high as possible. There should be no intermediate 'recovery' bounce.
8. *Arm Swinging.* Stand with your feet apart. Bring one arm forward, up past the ear, then as far back as possible and continue down in a circular motion. Repeat and gradually increase the speed. Do about 15 revolutions and then repeat with your other arm. Finish by circling both arms simultaneously.
9. *Small Jumps.* Do a series of small jumps, where most of the work is done by the feet and lower legs only. The knees should bend only slightly. This exercise can be done on both feet or only one foot at a time. (See illustration 6.)

Group Two
Specific strength and fitness training exercises
Fitness is a popular concept used to describe a condition of good health and reasonable athletic ability. For training purposes, however, this concept is too general. Fitness is specific to an activity. For example, a professional footballer may play his first game of tennis of the season only to find that his arm is stiff and aches the following day. He is fit for football, but is he fit for tennis?

Various factors contribute to athletic fitness. These include skill and agility, but the most important are *stamina, muscular endurance* and *strength.*

Stamina can be thought of as the ability of the whole body to *sustain* considerable effort and then to recover quickly in order to be able to repeat the effort if required.

Muscular endurance can be considered as similar to stamina, but applying only to particular muscle groups. This aspect of fitness is most relevant to fitness for skiing.

Strength is defined as the capacity of a muscle or muscle group to exert a force to overcome a resistance.

Maximum strength is achieved by moving against great resistance, for a small number of repetitions, whereas muscular endurance is achieved by making a larger number of repetitions with a lesser load. In this respect, training for strength or muscular endurance will have an effect on stamina

6. *Jeannine Spencer demonstrating 'small jumps'*

also, though this is best improved by total body exercises such as those listed in the first part of *Group One*.

Exercises for Group Two

1. *Squat Jumps.* Clasp hands on head with your right foot forward and left foot back, make a *half* knee bend. Jump explosively upwards, change position of feet in the air, and land with left foot forward and right foot back. Continue jumping without pause.

7.   *Squat jumps*

2. *Press-ups*. Lie on stomach, hands by your shoulders and your chin very near the floor. You must hold your hips off the floor and keep your whole body rigid. Now straighten your arms!

8. *Press-up*

9. *Press-up from knees*

10. *Press-ups. Raise your feet to increase the load*

Lower yourself in control and repeat. If you cannot manage even one press-up, and many people cannot, you may keep your knees on the floor. When you can manage over 40 press-ups, raise your feet and so increase the load.

3. *Box Jump.* Stand on one side of a stool or small box. Jump sideways over the stool, land on other side and take off again immediately. Continue without stopping or pausing.

11.
Box jump

4. *Sit-ups.* Lie on back with hands behind head and legs bent. Sit up to touch your elbow against the opposite knee, lie down carefully. Repeat to other side (see illustration 12).

When you can do 40 repetitions change to 'V' sit-ups.

V sit-ups. Lie flat on back, arms outstretched. Keep legs straight and sit up with a quick pike action to touch toes, return carefully to starting position (see illustration 13 opposite).

12.   *Sit-ups*

13.   *'V'-sits*

5. *Trunk Lift*. Lie on your stomach. Clasp your hands behind your head and brace your feet under a heavy weight or piece of furniture, or use a partner or coach to hold your feet down. Lift your upper body as high as possible.

14. *Trunk lifts with a partner holding feet down*

6. *Step-ups.* Stand with your feet together, in front of a box, chair or stool. Step onto the box, stand completely upright, then step down until both feet are on the floor. Repeat.

15. *Step-ups*

7. *Reverse Press-up.* Put your hands on a steady table or box, etc., behind you. Bend your arms and lower yourself down slowly, as far as you can. Straighten your arms keeping your body as rigid as you can. (See illustration **16** below.)

8. *Lateral Raise.* Lie on your side with your feet against a wall, etc. Straighten your right arm beneath you and then raise your hips as high as you can, in the same plane as the body.
(See illustration **17** below.)

9. *Handstand*. This exercise will improve balance and shoulder strength but should not be attempted in a confined space.

18.   *Handstand*

10. *Burpee*. Crouch down and put your palms on the floor either side of
    your knees. In one movement, jump backwards in a 'press-up'
    position; in a second movement, jump forwards again to start
    position. Repeat without pausing.
    (See illustration **19** above.)

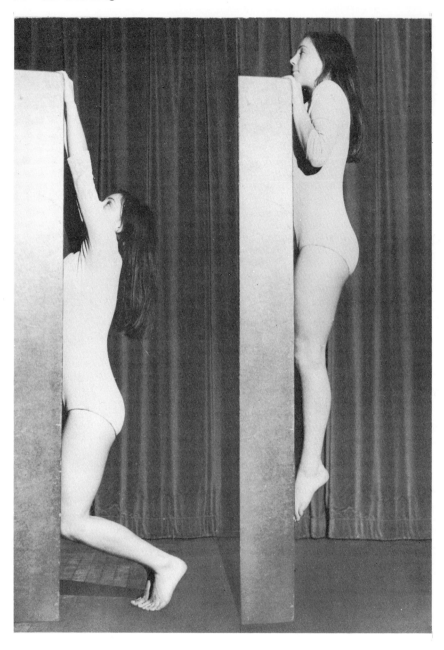

11. *Pull-up*. Hang with straight arms from the top of a cupboard, door or other suitable object. Using only your arms, pull up until your chin reaches your hands. Lower yourself slowly.
(See illustration **20** above.)

12. *Single Leg Squats*. Stand on your right foot. Hold your left leg out straight in front of you. Lower yourself carefully by bending your right leg. If you can do this exercise without lifting your heel, do so. Straighten up again in balance. Repeat with the left leg after training dose. Bend your leg to 90° only.
(See illustration **21** above.)

Group Three
Flexibility and mobility exercises
These exercises are designed to increase the range of movements of your joints and to increase your agility. Some of the exercises could cause strain in ligaments and tendons. The exercises *must* therefore be done slowly without any hurried or jerky movements. All exercises should be attempted by sustained pressure stretching and *not* by using body weight and momentum to 'bounce' and stretch. Prolonged tension in one muscle group will cause *Reciprocal Innervation* in the antagonist (opposite) group, allowing this group to stretch while relaxed. This will be obtained by slow, firm presses at the extreme of the range of free movement in that joint.

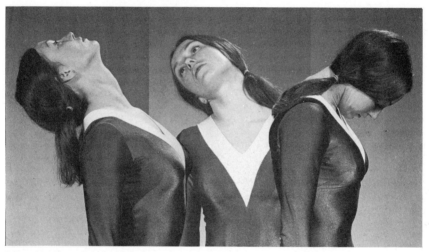

22.   *Neck circling*

Exercises for Group Three

1. *Neck Circling.* Move your head around as large a circle as you can, while keeping your shoulders still. Continue for about 20 seconds.

2. *Shoulder Stretch.* Hold your arms out to the side at shoulder length, your palms facing forward. Slowly, but firmly press your arms back as far as they will go. Hold that position and try to relax. Press arms back further, hold position and relax, press back again for approximately 10 seconds.

3. *Frontal Stretch.* Lie face downwards with your hands on the floor, close to your shoulders. Straighten your arms and, keeping your hips on the floor, try to raise your head as high and as far back as you can. Hold this position for approximately 10 seconds. Repeat.

23.   *Shoulder stretch*

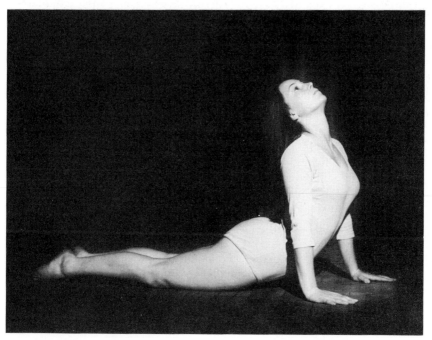

24.   *Frontal stretch*

4. *Crab Stand.* Lie on your back. Place your hands under your shoulders, and your feet close to your seat. Raise your body as high as you can by straightening your arms and legs. Hold this position for approximately 10 seconds. Relax and repeat. (See illustration **25** above.)

26. *Hip stretch*

5. *Hip Stretch*. Kneel with your lower legs parallel but about 18 inches apart. Try to sit down slowly onto the floor between your feet. (See illustration 26.)
6. *Hip and Knee Circling*. Stand upright with your feet about hip-width apart
   (a) Move your hips in as large horizontal circles as you can.
   (b) Move your knees in as large horizontal circles as you can.

27. *Hip circling*

28. *Knee circling*

7. *Back and Hamstring Stretch.* Sit on the floor with your legs straight out in front of you. Relax your lower back, reach forward and touch toes. Slowly try to touch your head on your knees. *Do not bounce.* When you can touch your head on your knees, sit with legs wide apart and straight, with toes pointed. Slowly reach forward to touch head onto floor.

29 & 30.
Back and hamstring stretch

31.   *Thigh, hip and abdominal stretch*

8. *Thigh, Hip and Abdominal Stretch*. Clasp your hands behind your head. Keeping your back upright, assume a lunge posture with your feet as far apart as you can. (Back and forth, not side to side). Press your hips down as low as you can.
(See illustration 31.)

9. *Diagonal Reach*. Stand on your toes with legs bent. Reach round and back with your right hand to touch the heel of your left foot. Hold it for up to five seconds.
(See illustration 32 opposite.)

32. *Diagonal reach*

Group Four
Equipment Familiarization Exercises
These exercises should be practised while wearing equipment. They are movements which will help you to get used to your 'new feet'. Many of these exercises will form part of your first lessons on the snow, where it will be necessary to move forwards, backwards and around obstacles before you can begin to learn to ski. If the skis you are using have steel edges, make sure that you do not damage the floor on which you are working.

Exercises for Group Four
1. *Lift feet alternately.* Keep your skis parallel to the floor. Try not to use sticks for balance.
2. Tap the tip of your left ski on either side of your right ski. Repeat with the right ski. Aim for speed and accuracy.
3. Balance on one foot and draw circles in the air with the tip of the other ski. (For variety, write your name, etc.)

4. Support yourself on the left side, by leaning on your ski sticks. Keeping your legs straight, lift your right ski as high as you can, keeping it horizontal. Practice left and right.
5. Stand with your feet hip-width apart. Skip jump with a firm spring and a gentle landing. Aim for a *complete leg extension*.
6. Begin as above. Spring and bring your feet together, spring again from a feet together stance, and land as you began. Continue with an easy rhythm, trying to keep your skis parallel.
7. Begin exercise as above, but now try to hop in and out of a 'V' shape (i.e. heels together), then an 'A' shape (tips together). Continue rhythmically, eventually springing from an 'A' to a 'V' back to an 'A', etc.
8. Keep your feet parallel and slide your left and right feet forwards and backwards, alternately.
9. *Walking and Gliding*. Do not lift your feet as you walk forward. Lean into the direction of movement with your whole body, and use your arms naturally to place the sticks by your feet and push yourself forwards.

33.   *Colin Whiteside 'walking on the level'*

10. *Step or clock turns* (sometimes known as star turns). Stand with your skis together. Keep your tips together and step around to the left (or right) in a series of 'A' shapes. Similarly, you can keep the heels of the skis together and make a series of 'V' steps. A combination of 'A's

and 'V's will enable you to turn around in a smaller area than if the tips or heels alone are used as pivot points.

11. Keep your skis parallel and step sideways. By kneeling and pushing off your toes you will begin to acquire a feeling for the 'edges' of the skis. Develop the sideways step into a running movement. Ensure that you always bend your legs at the *ankles* as well as the knees.

12. *Basic Shuss posture.* Stand with your feet hip width apart and with your skis parallel. Bend a little at the ankles, knees and hips. You should hold your hands about hip height, forward and to the side of your body, with the sticks pointing backwards and diverging slightly. You should try to feel that weight is being supported by the whole of your feet. Do not stand on your heels alone.
(See illustration 32.) This posture is basic for maintaining balance on your first downhill runs.

Note for Pre-Ski Instructors
In organizing pre-ski classes, you should use imagination and games, relay races, etc. to increase the students' enjoyment of all these exercises, but especially those in *Group Four.*

Circuit Training

The most effective form that pre-ski training sessions can take is that of *Circuit Training.* This system was developed in Great Britain by Morgen and Adamson at Leeds University in the early 1950s. Since that time, it has been used successfully all over the world by competitive as well as purely recreational athletes. It is a system for developing all round fitness, i.e. stamina, muscular endurance and strength. It is ideally suited for pre-ski training when no special equipment is available, because it enables all individuals to work hard at their own level, without having to keep up with, or hold back for, others. The system is also suitable for pre-ski training because very little skill is needed to perform the exercises.

The term 'circuit' refers to a series of exercises which are performed one after another without pause. In the case of pre-ski training, exercises for the circuit should be selected from *Group Two.*

The circuit will, however, only be part of your training sessions. You should begin each session by warming up (exercises from *Group One*). This will increase your circulation and initial mobility in anticipation of the exercise ahead.

After the circuit, with its emphasis on strength and endurance training, you should practise stretching and relaxing, using exercises from *Group Three.* These exercises are among the most important, though sadly often the most neglected. When you work your muscles in a serious training session, they tend to shorten, become bulky and lose a little elasticity. The movements of your joints may be slightly restricted. *Group Three* exercises will counter this effect.

A skier with good mobility will be less likely to be injured in a fall than one who is very strong but lacks flexible joints. Good mobility has the effect of giving you confidence and thereby enables you to learn to ski with less effort and with an increased sense of freedom and exhilaration.

Organizing the Circuit
(a)   Select between five and ten exercises from *Group Two*. Those selected must include different body-part emphases, i.e. legs, arms, trunk.
(b)   List these exercises so that different body parts are exercised successively.
(c)   Study the exercises and the illustrations carefully, and try to do each one correctly. Once you have mastered each exercise, you are ready to work out your training programme.
(d)   Perform the first exercise of your selection by doing as many correct repetitions of it as you can. Record the result on a card (see illustration 34) in the column marked 'MAX.' (for maximum). Take a rest. Find your maximum number of repetitions for the second exercise and mark your card. Repeat this procedure for all the exercises you have selected.
(e)   When you have recorded your maximum score for each exercise, complete your card by inserting in the column marked 'TR' (for training repetitions) *half* your maximum score for each exercise. You are now ready to begin your circuit-training sessions. Work your way *three* times around the circuit, using your training dose (TR) at each exercise. That is, if the maximum number of press-ups you could manage was six then your training dose will be three.

Do each repetition of each exercise correctly, and move from one exercise to the next without resting.

You should feel that the third time around the circuit really puts you under 'load'.

Do not rush the exercises, but remember to keep good form. Record your total time for all three circuits.

Your increase in strength and fitness will be reflected in the time that it takes you to complete the circuits at subsequent training sessions.

Target Time
You should aim, at a later training session, to complete your circuit in your target time. This should be 80 per cent of the initial time for your three circuits.

When your target time is reached, retest yourself for your maximum repetitions in each exercise and adjust the training doses on your card accordingly – on the second and third columns your target time should be 90 per cent of the initial time for that circuit.

When you have reached your third target time, either add an extra exercise (if training time permits), or change your circuit exercises for similar ones, e.g. step-ups for squat jumps and sit-ups for 'V'-sits.

Sample Score Card

NAME	William B. A. Skier.					
DATE	5th Aug. '79.					
EXERCISES	MAX.	T R.	MAX.	T R.	MAX.	T R.
1. Step ups	49	25				
2. Press ups	20	10				
3. Trunk lifts	60	30				
4. Box jumps	60	30				
5. Sit ups	30	15				
6. Burpees	32	16				
7.						
INITIAL TIME .	12 min. 10 sec.		min. sec.		min. sec	
Intermediate Circuit TIMES	1 12 min 3	9	1	9	1	9
	2 11m. 56	10	2	10	2	10
	3 11m. 41.	11	3	11	3	11
	4 11m. 19.	12	4	12	4	12
	5 11m. 3.	13	5	13	5	13
	6 10m. 40	14	6	14	6	14
	7	15	7	15	7	15
	8	16	8	16	8	16
TARGET TIME	80% 9 min 42s		90%		90%	

34. *Sample score card*

In all exercises where your initial maximum score is greater than 30, determine your 'maximum' by how many you can do in *one minute*, that is, your 'maximum' will be either how many repetitions you can manage altogether, or in one minute, whichever comes first.

Conclusion
At the end of each training session, controlled breathing can help to calm you down and provide a very satisfactory conclusion to your period of exercise.

Controlled Breathing Exercise
Sit comfortably near a source of fresh air, preferably on a cushion, with forearms resting on knees, back upright. Keep your shoulders low. Breathe out gently until your lungs are almost empty. Breathing through the nose, draw in air along the roof of the nose, down the back of the

throat and down into the lower region of the lungs; and then in a second movement, allow the top half of the lungs to fill and the rib cage to rise and expand. Hold your breath for a second or two. Breathe out slowly and completely by forcing the air out from the bottom of the lungs. Continue the breathing cycle, and try to match the duration of your exhaling phase to that of your inhaling phase. Try to relax your body, keep your shoulders low and feel all your weight being carried by the spine to the hips. Focus your attention on your breath, imagine it flowing in, flowing out. Do not allow your mind to wander. Close your eyes and 'watch' your breathing.

Complete success will not be achieved immediately, but eventually you will be able to calm yourself after exercise, or prior to competition, easily and effectively with this exercise.

If you ski competitively, this exercise can help you to calm your mind before the start of a race. Try to remain relaxed, concentrate on the run ahead, and if you feel excitement rising return your attention to your breathing rhythm. Deep controlled breathing can be extremely beneficial while you are in the start gate.

Diet

For maximum enjoyment of and performance in your skiing, you should try to maintain a reasonable level of fitness all year round. Good exercise and breathing habits should be developed and you should select a nutritious diet. It is not normally necessary to 'go on a diet'; care in selection of your everyday foods will suffice. A brief guide is given below:

Eat sparingly	Foods to eat
White sugar and jam	Honey
White bread	Whole grain bread, rye bread
Cakes, biscuits and pastry	Sultanas, raisins, all dried fruits, peanuts
Chocolate and sweets	Almonds, cashews, Brazil nuts, etc.
Spaghetti and macaroni	Meat, fish, poultry, eggs, cheese, liver and kidney
Concentrated sugar drinks	Pure fruit juices, fresh fruit, milk
Sugar-frosted and chocolate-coated breakfast cereals	Porridge and honey

General Rules

Boiled food is generally better than fried food. Steamed or grilled food is easier to digest and fat should be eaten sparingly. It is, however, important to enjoy your food, especially on holiday. It is very doubtful if you will benefit a great deal from eating food you do not like, just because it is considered 'healthy' to do so.

It must be realized that good general fitness cannot be achieved without some measure of hard work. There is no short-cut to 'getting fit'. Therefore when you are 'fit', it is worth maintaining your condition by observing the factors which influence fitness.

These factors include those that I have mentioned already, i.e. your general health, diet and level of activity, and one that I have not mentioned before, the amount of sleep that you have. This is a most important factor, especially when you are on holiday and tempted to ski all day and dance all night. A ski holiday should be a lot of fun, and to make the most of your night-life you might like to consider resting or sleeping from four or five o'clock until dinner time. Many skiers find that this helps them to get the best of both worlds.

A Sample Pre-Ski Training Schedule

To be performed twice a week for three months before the winter season begins, and once per week for the rest of the year.

The outline of the training sessions applies to individuals working alone or in a group.

1. *Initial Activity*   2–4 minutes. Warming up.
   Three or four exercises from *Group One*. (Vary the exercises at each training session to add interest and variety.)
2. *Fitness Training Circuit*   9–14 minutes.
   Select between 5 and 10 exercises from *Group Two*, and practise as described previously. A suggested series of exercises is as follows:

   1. Step-ups
   2. Press-ups
   3. Trunk lift   to begin with if you are not very fit.
   4. Box jump
   5. Sit-ups
   6. Burpees
   7. Reverse press-ups
   8. Squat jumps   to add when you want to train hard.
   9. Pull-ups
   10. Single leg squats

   At the end of the circuit do not sit or lie down, even though you will feel exhausted. Walk slowly around and 'limber' down.
3. *Flexibility Training* for 4 or 5 minutes after 'limbering' down. Select 4 to 6 exercises from *Group Three* and perform 4 to 6 repetitions of each.

If you have worked hard at your training session you will feel hot, thirsty and tired. Do not eat or drink very much immediately you have finished training. Take a short walk, well wrapped up to keep warm, and then have a light meal and drink if you wish.

Over the total period of your training schedule, ensure that your liquid intake is adequate, and ensure that it remains so when you go skiing. It is relatively easy to become dehydrated in the dry air on an energetic Alpine ski holiday.

CHAPTER THREE

Skill in Skiing on Artificial Slopes

It is generally accepted that walking and running are natural movements of man. These are normal developments which occur during maturation. Skiing is not one of man's innate abilities: it is an ability which has to be learned. As such, its acquisition can be affected by the conditions under which it is learned. That is to say, the environment and method of learning are more or less conducive to the successful acquisition of skilful performance in skiing.

It has been said that 'physical skills cannot be learned without having a go!' In order to learn to ski, one must ski, that is, one must slide down a mountainside under the influence of gravity. It might appear at first sight that the obvious thing to do then, if one wants to learn to ski, is to find a pair of skis and then, as Mrs Beaton would say, 'Find your mountain'. This is certainly the traditional approach and one which has been quite successful for many skiers over the years. But with the advent of artificial ski slopes, we now have a more suitable alternative to the mountain, though the suitability of an artificial ski slope will depend very much upon its design.

Artificial ski slopes were invented to enable skiers to practice their sport. They were designed to ski on and not specifically to learn to ski on. In Britain it has been found that after the initial use of the first ski slopes by competent skiers, the greatest use of such slopes is made by beginners. People who do not ski well or even at all, but who would like to ski, take the opportunity to learn to do so locally, before embarking upon voyages to foreign climes.

The change in usage of artificial ski slopes has been recognized, but in too few cases have the implications of this change been seen.

Too many slopes are still too steep and with too little run out space. To be most satisfactory for beginners to learn on, the run out area must be considered as important as the slope.

The area at the bottom of the slope should be flat and, if possible, have a slight counterslope at one side, opposing the main slope. This will ensure that the beginner can run down the main slope in safety and comfort without having to stop, and, more important, without being concerned with how to stop.

Although the cost of such an area increases the cost of the slope, it does mean that more beginners can be moving (and therefore learning) at any one time, and classes can be bigger than if the slope only allowed one person to be moving at any one time. Examples of very good 'run out' areas can be seen at:

Plas y Brennin; Madeley Court, Telford; The Oval, Bebington and the new slope at Aviemore (see illustration 35).

35.   *The good 'run out' area on the new Aviemore ski slope*

It may seem strange to say that it is possible to learn to ski more efficiently on a well-designed artificial slope than it is on an open mountainside, but this is so. It is due to the nature of the activity itself.

Psychologists who have studied physical activities have classified and divided them into two general categories – 'closed' or 'open'. Activities are termed closed when the learner builds patterns of movement techniques, which are as close to the theoretical ideal for his build as possible, and which are performed without reference to his external environment (that is, without requiring external stimulus for their performance). An example of a closed skill is putting the shot.

Open skills, on the other hand, are 'skills in which the techniques being performed have to fit either an unpredictable series of environmental requirements, or a very exacting series, whether predictable or unpredictable'. (*Poulton* from *Knapp* page 151). Association football is an example of an open skill, but there are other complex skills which cannot be neatly classified either as open or closed. Skiing is one.

Skiing is an activity which is more open than closed. During a run down a mountainside, gradient and speed, snow texture and resistance, terrain and weather, will all alter, and will demand appropriate responses from the skier if he is to remain in complete control of himself. He has to be constantly adapting himself to rapidly changing circumstances.

The techniques which will be used to maintain control in a descent must be performed as efficiently and as automatically as possible; the skier's attention will be directed to the changing conditions with which he must cope, and it is this that makes skiing hard to learn. The beginner does not have a repertoire of techniques which he can use automatically, and yet, while trying to learn these techniques, he still has to cope with a continuously changing slope. His problems are further increased by the fact that, once he is on the slope, he has to make positive actions even to remain still. He cannot rest or relax completely as this would cause him to slide downhill, and thus require him to use those techniques which he has not yet learned.

It is reasonable, therefore, to begin learning to ski on a well chosen slope, with as many of the external variables as possible either minimized or removed completely. A well designed artificial ski slope can provide a learning area which is far more suitable than a snow slope in this respect. The beginner can then concentrate on learning the basic techniques (the closed aspects of skiing) on a constant, predictable surface in comparative safety and comfort, without having to modify these movements, before he has fully mastered them, in order to remain in control of himself and his equipment. As the beginner's technical proficiency increases, his environment can be 'opened' in a controlled manner by the introduction of artificial 'moguls' or bumps, which have to be skied over, or slalom poles which must be skied around, etc. There is naturally a limit to the amount of variety that can be introduced in this manner, and for this reason artifical ski slopes could never become a substitute for open snow.

The place of the artificial ski slope is to provide a medium on which beginners can learn the basic techniques of skiing, and on which more advanced skiers can isolate particular problems and practice techniques which will enable them to cope with these problems when they return to the snow.

The position which skiing occupies in the continuum between open and closed skills has positive implications for the design of training. The closed aspects of the skill require considerable time and effort to be spent on building basic patterns of movement, called *Motor Techniques*, and a well designed artificial ski slope is possibly the most suitable place for doing this. On the other hand, the open aspects of the skill require that a great deal of attention be paid to signals from the external environment, and to the judgements and decisions which have to be made. Such perceptual skills can, in the main, only be developed effectively through practice on open terrain.

The truly skilled skier will be one who has a considerable range of motor techniques and perceptual abilities at his command, and who is able to use them according to the situation.

When the beginner has mastered the techniques described in the Ground School, he will be able to travel safely on open terrain where his momentum will have more relevance to his movements than his static weight.

Learning is achieved by modifying that which you can do already, and so to develop skiing abilities beyond the basics the skier must increase the variety of terrain over which he skis and increase his speed while still maintaining control. Balance and posture are interrelated and just as balance must be adjusted from stationary positions and very slow speeds to turning at higher speeds, so one's posture must adjust to cope most effectively with the new stresses, demands and opportunities that extra speed and momentum bring.

36.   *Martin Bell, British Junior Champion, shows excellent posture at speed*
   Note :   1. Quiet head.
   2. Arms. Quiet, forward with loose shoulders
   3. Angulation at hips

As the steepness of the slope and speed increase, the 'feeling of weight' against the feet will diminish and movements become possible which cannot even be attempted while standing still. This is the world of truly dynamic skiing, which encompasses the popular skiing images of high speed Alpine racing and of 'floating through the deep powder'.

The techniques of the Ground School will put the beginner in touch with this world.

37. *Hans Kuwall shows excellent posture. Compare with Martin Bell: loose but perfectly controlled arms, diverging sticks and hip angulation*

38.   *Ingemar Stenmark, Triple World Cup Winner, has perfectly disciplined posture and arm control even when he is 'free skiing'*

CHAPTER FOUR

The Ground School of Skiing

'The Design of Training' or the Construction of a Syllabus from a Skill Analysis of Skiing

The syllabus which follows has been designed especially for use on a suitable artificial ski slope: that is, one which has a smooth and constant surface, a smooth transition onto a flat run out area which, for preference, has a slight counterslope opposing the main slope. It is equally suitable for use on any snow slope which has been carefully selected and groomed with the requirements of beginners in mind.

The method is not concerned directly with the more advanced techniques of 'jet' turns or *avalement*, but it confines itself to the *fundamental* techniques which are required by every skier to control himself and his equipment while moving on a slope under the direct influence of gravity. Once mastered, these fundamental techniques can be developed according to the physical abilities and personal requirements of the student. They will give him sufficient control, in dynamic situations, over individual body parts and his equipment to enable him to extend his skill in any direction he chooses, and to respond to the directions of any future ski teacher he may have without having to 'unlearn' or break down previous learning.

The techniques are basic to all ski teaching systems and if attention is given to these techniques and not to the individual style of the instructor, the student should have very few problems if he should change instructors during the early stages of learning.

The teaching method has been designed from an analysis of all the skills used by expert skiers negotiating open terrain, and after consideration of factors which affect the acquisition of these skills by beginners.

The Analysis of Skiing Abilities

In general terms a skill analysis should contain the following information:
1. A description of the movements involved in the skilled performance.

The combinations, the sequences, the speed and degree of effort in the movements must all be noted.

2. A breakdown of the primary control senses for the identified movements.

39.   *Skill analysis: photomontage shows Roddy Langmuir, British Senior Squad, carving a turn on an artificial ski slope. Hip angulation, leg rotation, refined edge changing and many other aspects of technique can be clearly seen*

The movements are known as *Motor Techniques* and the sensory controls are known as *Perceptual Abilities.*

Such an analysis of skiing is not easy. There are many difficulties, some of which are mentioned here briefly.

The speed and variety of the movements are problems, but the use of film and photographs can give considerable help here. (See illustrations 40 and 41.) The second problem arises when the observations are interpreted in different ways by different observers, though a logical approach with knowledge of mechanical and anatomical principles helps in this case.

The perceptual abilities are equally problematic. The sensory cues are difficult to locate accurately, and the personal impressions of the performer have largely to be relied upon. Personal involvement by the observer has helped here.

'Blanking off' and eliminating senses one at a time and in pairs have yielded a considerable amount of information about perpetual abilities in

40. *Skill analysis: as Hayden Scott starts a new turn, it can be seen that his legs rotate back into the 'line of the hips and torso' as his angulation decreases*

skiing, though there is still a lot of work which could be done in this field. The intricate details of the analysis of skiing abilities is inappropriate here, but the important techniques have been summarized below.

Basic Motor Techniques
1. Extension and flexion of legs, combined with loose, omnidirectional movements of hips and trunk, with appropriate angulation, to enable *Dynamic Balance* (or *Anticipatory Balance*) to be maintained.
2. Extension and flexion of legs, combined with appropriate angulation to enable *Pressure* against different parts of the skis to be changed.
3. Control of Edging.
4. Rotation of legs to produce steering of both skis independently though often simultaneously.

Perceptual Abilities
1. Recognition of movement.
   (a) Personal movement within the body. This involves awareness of body tensions, distribution of effort in movements, awareness of 'body shape' and of the pressures under the feet during weight transference (*Proprioception*).
   (b) Movement of the skier over the terrain. This involves awareness, through visual, auditory and tactile clues, of rate of movements in relation to the terrain.

41. *Skill analysis: as Per Gwalter angulates to control his turn, the forward flex at the hips and rotation (with abduction and flexion) of the legs can be clearly seen*

The perceptual process which results from combining (a) and (b) above is known as *Kinaesthesis*.

2. Recognition of terrain. This aspect of perceptual skill enables the appropriate responses to be made in suitable places in a suitable manner. This is essentially visual, though auditory and proprioceptive clues contribute to this skill. For example, a skier moving off soft snow onto either ice or wind-crusted snow should be able to recognize the

change in terrain by visual clues and also by the changes in 'feeling under foot' and the sounds that his skis make as they slide on the snow. Changes in sight, sound and feeling occur continuously, not only when changing from one snow texture to another, but throughout every turn as movement and pressure changes occur between the skis and the snow. These changes give information both about the rate of movement (1b) and the nature of the terrain (2).

Note: The value of tactile, auditory and kinaesthetic clues is sometimes underestimated by ski instructors who often fail to recognize their importance. The artificial ski slope, which is noisier and has 'more feel' than normal piste, can increase a skier's awareness of the role of hearing and 'feeling with the feet' in developing skilled performances.

An outstanding characteristic of modern ski techniques is the dominant position occupied by the legs and the feet as initiators and controllers of movement. Movements of the upper body are made only when they can help the legs to do their work. In this respect, clarity of intention and a relaxed upper body are essential to gain maximum effect from the use of the legs.

The Teaching Method

'All learning affects the learning which follows.'

The syllabus has been designed to synthesize fundamental techniques. They build to form composite techniques which will transfer directly from the closed environment of the nursery slope to the open terrain. They should never be learned as isolated movements merely for their immediate results, and their relationship to the whole skill should always be considered. For example, if side-slipping is to be learned in order to be able to lose height on a slope, then the particular technique used is not very important because one of many will suffice. But if it is to be learned as an integral part of most skiing turns, then the technique learned must be side-skidding, under the influence of momentum, which will transfer directly into the skiing turns that will be learned later. It is of little use learning to slip sideways, using straight legs in a high stance with skis almost totally flattened to the slope, if the turns to be learned later require the skis to be 'edged' and the legs to be bent.

Whenever a choice of techniques is available to overcome immediate problems, the technique which is safest and has the most opportunities for learning should be used. In skiing terms, the teaching method will take the beginner from his first steps on level ground through *Basic Swing Turning* to basic parallel turns, whenever this is appropriate.

The exercise plan which follows indicates desirable progressions of learning. It is a guide to be used with imagination and intelligence. It should not be considered as an inflexible set of rules to be followed blindly without due consideration for the needs of individual students.

The Teaching Method In Terms of the Skill Analysis

The basic abilities to be learned are cumulative, and overlapping.
1. Control of body and equipment (in non-sliding and in basic sliding, slipping and skidding situations).
2. Dynamic balance.
3. Control of Skidding + Dynamic balance.
4. Steering + Skidding + Dynamic balance.
5. Weight or pressure changing + Steering + Skidding + Dynamic balance.
6. Basic perceptual skills.

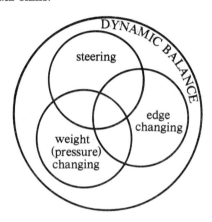

The four factors shown in the diagram are fundamental requirements in any and all skiing turns and may be performed more or less skilfully and may, therefore, be termed 'fundamental skiing skills'.

While all changes of direction of travel, i.e. all turns, incorporate these 'fundamental skills', they will not occur in the same temporal sequence for all skiing turns. Indeed, learning the 'fundamental skills' and then changing their sequence of application within a turn will determine the nature of that turn.

Skidding or braking turns will be characterized by steering and edge changing followed by pressure changing, whereas 'carved', or sliding, non-braking turns are characterized by a different sequence of the fundamental skills in any such turn, i.e. weight or pressure change, followed by edge changing and steering with refined dynamic balance contribute to 'carved' turns.

The advantages of considering skiing in terms of these 'fundamental skills' are as follows:
1. The conceptual complexity of skiing is reduced.
2. Steering, edging, pressure control are all subject to 'proprioceptive feedback'. The skier can feel and experience them, learning to regulate their intensity of application through this 'feedback loop'.

3. All technical problems can be traced to the need for improvement in one or more of these four simply recognized areas.
4. Learners' practices become more meaningful as they concentrate on increasing their awareness of movements and their inextricable consequences, rather than working on body movement patterns in isolation.
5. Learning can develop according to skiers' aims, and more advanced techniques can be learned by altering the application sequence of these 'fundamental skiing skills.'

In Skiing Terms
1. Equipment familiarization exercises. Walking, turning, moving up/down slope, turning on the slope.
2. Basic Shussing.
3. Side-skidding controls. Ploughing.
4. Traversing and uphill swing. Plough turns and plough swings.
   Basic Swing Turning.
5. The basic swing turns allow dynamic skiing in open terrain in order to develop the perceptual skills which will 'open' the skier's skill. The basic swing turns will lead to parallel turning in open terrain which can be developed further to suit the aims of individual students.

CHAPTER FIVE

Principles of Ski Teaching

'The art of teaching a skill is very different from the art of performing that skill.'

In this chapter I shall attempt to outline some of the basic principles of teaching: primarily to provide a sound basis on which the student ski instructor can develop his art, but also in the hope that it will give all skiers some insight into their learning and thereby help them to gain maximum benefit from instruction and training.

The Role of the Ski Instructor

The instructor is the leader and motor of his class. He is responsible for his students' safety and well-being, for their enjoyment and their learning. Their activities should always be planned in relation to these priorities.

A good instructor will keep up to date in his knowledge of new techniques and teaching methods, and be able to determine how these apply to his particular teaching situation. He must also have some knowledge of psychology and learning processes; but most important of all, he must be competent in, and have a sound knowledge of, the skills and techniques that he is going to teach. He must have a real desire to impart this knowledge to his students, and be able to do so with *empathy*. 'The teacher possesses the art of approaching the subject from the point of view of the beginner. He is able to enter into the psychological situation of one encountering the subject for the first time.' (From *Introduction To Thomas Aquinas* by Joseph Pieper.)

In order to create and maintain his image as a respectable and professional person, the ski instructor should always be suitably dressed, clean, tidy, and well equipped. Any waterproof overgarments which might be worn in inclement weather should not be too bulky. They should not detract from the body lines, because he must ensure that demonstrations are as clear as possible.

The overall success of any instructional session is ultimately determined by how much the students enjoy the activity and how enthusiastic they are to continue with it. In this respect, the ski intructor's technical knowledge will be of little value unless his personal manner enables him to communicate this knowledge effectively. If the instructor is concerned with beginners, it is likely that his friendliness, sense of humour and above all his patience, will not only determine how much they learn from his instruction, but will also affect their whole attitude towards learning and skiing generally.

The Instruction

The need to build solid foundations for students' progress and avoid bad habits means that the students should have expert instruction from the very beginning. Indeed this is probably more important at this stage of learning than at any other.

Careful thought and preparation are essential if good results are to be obtained.

Preparation

1. The Group

Who is to be taught? The lessons will need to be geared to the make-up of the group members, depending upon their age, and the range of abilities within the group.

How many are there? Depending upon available, safe terrain, up to eight is ideal and twenty should be considered a maximum.

Why are they learning? The approach to teaching will vary, depending upon the reasons for the students' attendance. These may be educational, for serious training or purely recreational.

2. The Subject

What is to be taught? Bear in mind:
The terrain available,
the time available, and
the learning capacities of the students.
(Beware of flooding the beginner with too much information. It is better to teach a little well, than a lot badly.)
And *always progress from the known to the unknown.*

3. The Equipment

Ensure that sufficient equipment in a serviceable condition is ready beforehand.

Skis

These should have a sound running-surface with all edges intact. They should be shorter than normal, approx. 150–170 cm for absolute beginners, and on no account should they be longer than the student's own height.

Bindings
Both toe and heel bindings should have release mechanisms. These should be checked for smooth operation (usually by the person responsible for hiring them out). They should be 'set' lightly for beginners, in relation to their weight and strength. In any event, it is a good practice for each student to twist his toe iron to both sides before each practice period to ascertain that it will release in an emergency. Retaining straps need not be worn on small slopes, but are essential on large slopes or on snow.

Boots
These should be of accepted design, offering good lateral support, yet permitting forward movement of the lower legs. They should be as comfortable as possible.

Sticks
These should be as light as possible. They should have handles though the straps need not be used: on some artificial slopes, the stick may get stuck in the slope and pull the student over if he cannot let go completely.

The ideal length for the sticks is from ground to elbow when the student stands completely upright. Absolute beginners may find that slightly longer sticks will give them more purchase when walking and climbing.

Teaching Aids
Whistle.
Flags/slalom poles.
Small bumps. (These can be portable on an artificial slope or built with a shovel on the snow.)
An easy tow. This is not part of an instructor's personal equipment, but every opportunity should be taken to use a ski tow if it will increase the amount of downhill skiing that the students can do in any given period of instruction.
Dye. A bottle of water dye is very useful on the snow for marking the boundaries of the practice area or illustrating the fall line, etc. Many pupils have difficulty in their early lessons, in controlling their skis. This may not be because of their inability to perform the required technique but because of their inability to *perceive* precisely *what* is required and *where*, with sufficient accuracy. As beginners they are learning to operate in a strange, tilted, slippy and relatively featureless environment, which contrasts strongly with the familiar, flat, sticky and regularly marked pavements, floors, etc., of the normal world.

The use of dye lines to mark exactly where the skis should run in such turns as snowplough turns can aid pupils' perceptions of the tasks considerably.

42.   *The use of dye lines can aid the pupils' perceptions of the task*

4. The Terrain
The minimum gradient conducive to easy sliding for the relevant exercise should be used. An adequate run out on a flat or slightly uphill counterslope is essential to enable the student to develop confidence and non-defensive postures.

The slope surface should be checked for loose corners, etc. Snow should be well pisted. When the available slope is large, up and down limits should be set to contain the group within a safe and manageable area.

5. Clothing
All students should wear adequate protective clothing, appropriate to the prevailing weather conditions, and for protection against abrasions from the artificial slope's surface. For the beginner, this should include strong trousers, long-sleeved shirt or pullover, and gloves or mitts.

6. *Safety*

The ski instructor must show authority and insist that the rules which he imposes are obeyed. (To be effective, such rules must be clear, precise and kept to a minimum.) Prevention is better than cure. The majority of accidents to beginners can be avoided, if adequate attention is paid to clothing, safety, etc., and provided a warming-up period, suitable to the age, experience and ability of the pupils, and the prevailing weather conditions, is given before the lesson begins.

In the event of an accident, the instructor should know where the first aid facilities and nearest telephone are. He should be able to administer simple first aid for bruises, cuts, etc., and must arrange for expert diagnosis of any suspected fracture. Serious sprains, twists and knocks should be treated as possible fractures and dealt with accordingly. If the injury occurs in the ankle region, the boot should not be removed as it will help support the joint and contain any swelling that might occur. While expert help is being summoned or first aid is being given, the injured student should be made as comfortable as possible and kept warm. He should not be given any alcoholic beverage.

The ski instructor is recommended to refer to the *First Aid* manuals of the St John's Ambulance Association, the St Andrew's Ambulance Association and the British Red Cross Society, and if possible to attend a training course given by any of these organizations.

Instruction Procedure

'Physical skills cannot be learned without "having a go" and few can be acquired at a single trial.' (Page 7, *Barbara Knapp*. Kegan Paul, London, 1963.)

It is very important to bear this in mind while both planning and giving instruction. The student learns to ski by skiing, i.e. as a result of his own experiences. While it is very necessary that the instructor demonstrates and explains what is to be learned, he should keep this to the minimum, thereby enabling the student to spend as much time as possible actually practising.

This practice, however, must be very carefully directed and guided by the instructor.

When a student learns to ski, he often starts with tremendous interest and enthusiasm. Early progress seems very rapid. Gradually the rate of improvement slows down and there may follow a period when no measureable learning takes place. Periods of this kind are known as *plateaux*. Improvement in the open aspects of the skill may be continued through this period, a sudden burst of progress will occur and carry the student forward again. But, it is worth noting, the *plateaux* often cause students to become so discouraged that they give up skiing. Since *plateaux* are discouraging, every effort should be made to avoid them, even if it means that initial progress is slower.

Four major causes of *plateaux* are:

1. Lack of enjoyment by the student.
2. Depression caused by the student's underestimation of his own progress.
3. Bad habits: incorrect movement patterns which have been acquired during early practice prevent further progress.
4. Methods of instruction which limit progress at a later date. Failure to learn a particular movement after continued attempts can cause an emotional blockage, marring the student's image of himself as a skier. Success, however limited, is essential and the ski instructor should make sure that he takes no action which will make a student anticipate failure.

It follows, therefore, that good form, i.e. techniques which are a good basis for further development, should be taught from the outset. The student should be able to see purpose in his efforts and the instructor should help him to appreciate his progress.

The form of the Instruction

(a) Explanation
(b) Demonstration   combined and repeated whenever necessary
(c) Imitation by the students
(d) Correction of faults
(e) Practice

(a) Explanation. This should be concise, and given in simple language.

Verbal instruction should be kept to a minimum, especially when dealing with beginners and young children. Long descriptions and the use of technical terms unfamiliar to the beginner may create a feeling of frustration, boredom and uncertainty, which may impede learning.

In an attempt to overcome some of these hazards, the descriptions in the teaching can be valuable when the student is no longer a beginner and is familiar with the technical terminology of the sport.

(b) Demonstration. This should be first class, with reasonable emphasis laid on the important aspects of the movement or position. If an exercise is shown in 'slow motion', it should be followed by a demonstration at the normal speed.

Kinaesthesis or 'movement sense' is very important in learning physical skills and many students will have the ability to watch a person perform and then do a somewhat similar action without necessarily bringing any conscious effort into it. (*Barbara Knapp.*)

For this reason the ski instructor should not demonstrate a refined 'examination style' performance but must demonstrate exactly what he expects the pupils to attempt. He must give them a goal which they can 'hit' first time and then improve on with subsequent attempts – 'we learn from our successes'. Most demonstrations should be given at normal speed to help the student get the 'feel' of the action.

Inherent in demonstrating 'parts' of a technique are dangers which the ski instructor should recognize. There is a tendency in such cases for the expert to demonstrate what he *thinks* is done instead of what actually happens when the total movement is made normally. These dangers can, to some extent, be avoided if knowledge of mechanical and anatomical principles is applied to acute observations. I refer especially to those observations made using high-speed photography and video-tape recorders, which enable the actions to be studied repeatedly, and which allow for analyses to be checked before a final demonstration form is decided upon.

In any demonstration, the quality and character of the movements are as important as the technical content. Rhythm, fluidity and effort qualities are all observed by the student and an indication of the importance of these should be given in subsequent explanations.

(c) Imitation. The students should attempt the movements as demonstrated.

Maximum activity of the whole class should be encouraged and the student's first attempts should be *reinforced* without any criticism. The instructor's approval will reinforce the learning. He should not expect his students to perform perfectly. He should accept *rough forms* and work steadily to improve these when the students have gained confidence and ability.

(d) Correction. While the students continue to practise, the instructor should help his pupils to correct their major faults first.

Remember this ... *Everything we do, works!*

Any pupil's response which is genuinely attempted has worked for him at that time. He has not done it wrongly (as he perceives it), but it is certain that it may be done more efficiently and effectively.

The Instructor should accept what his pupil does and encourage him to increase his own awareness of himself and his movements.

With patience and understanding he should attempt to modify *what he can do* and *is doing* into more efficient movements.

The instructor should not criticize unduly as this could prevent the student from attempting *any* movement from fear of failing. Comment should always be constructive. The instructor should indicate why a movement was not successful, and also how it could be improved.

Successful attempts should be reinforced. Praise will enable the student to recognize a successful movement, and so it follows that the instructor should praise good attempts more than he criticizes poor ones. Successful attempts should be repeated several times in order to further reinforce the correct action.

When giving praise, the instructor should always discriminate between praising the result or praising the effort. The student must know exactly what he is doing if learning is to be successful.

Corrections can be made only if the instructor has diagnosed the fault. It is not sufficient to know that something is wrong; the major fault must be determined and positive guidance given to correct it.

Irrespective of what exercise is being performed, or what level of skill the student has reached, the major fault can be determined by examining the performance in respect of the following questions.

Does the fault lie in his steering?
> edge change/edge control?
> weight (pressure) changing (method or amount)?
> OR
> Is the fault caused by a combination of one or more of these factors, related to poor *Dynamic Balance*?

1. Does the student have a loose, balanced posture?
2. Is he standing on his feet correctly?
3. Is he clear in his mind exactly what he is trying to do?
4. Is he defensive?
   Afraid of steepness,
   > speed,
   > exposure?

43.   *Does the pupil have a balanced posture, good control and a clear intention of what to attempt?*

44.   *In contrast to the beginner's stiff and awkward movements the balletic grace of the Freestyle skier has emerged as a new form of self-expression for expert skiers*

5. Is he in control of himself when he begins the manoeuvre?
6. Does he have any upper body mannerisms which hinder his leg action?
7. Is he simply making an incorrect response to the exercise?

When the faults have been determined, corrective guidance can be given as follows:

1. Work on one fault at a time. One major fault often causes many minor ones.
2. The instructor should try to correct by verbal guidance while the student continues to practise.
3. If verbal guidance does not succeed, then the fault will have to be isolated, and a demonstration of the fault may be necessary at this stage.
   (It is better to find a new exercise to overcome the fault than to persist in seeking success from the original one, when such attempts are merely reinforcing the incorrect movements.)
4. If these procedures fail to bring an improvement in the student's

performance, the instructor may have to resort to manual guidance, or stationary practices in non-sliding situations.

In such practices, where the instructor guides the actions of the student, and in some cases supplies the power too, the student must be encouraged to 'feel' for the correct action and supply the power himself as soon as possible.

5. In the event of all four methods of correction failing, the student should return to earlier, more familiar practices which will restore his self-confidence. A different approach to the task should then be attempted.

(e) Practice. Supervised, free practice of the activities taught should now be encouraged. Individual guidance in the open aspects of skiing skill can now be given to students, in addition to advice relating to minor faults.

Many pupils are not aware of the mistakes they make because they have poorly developed 'body awareness'. This 'sense', *Kinaesthesis*, can be sharpened by drawing students' attention to the 'feel' of the movements.

Kinaesthesis is the perceptual process which gives information about the shape of the body, relative positions of the limbs, and the strength of movements in these limbs. The other senses also provide valuable information which assists the skier in open aspects of his skill. These perceptual aspects of skiing skill can be developed if the instructor draws attention to the functions of the various senses while the student is actually practising.

We all learn and develop by modifying what we are doing. It follows that learning and development will be facilitated if we can increase our *awareness* of what (precisely) we are doing and what (precisely) is happening to us.

This *awareness* is feeling, not thinking and pupils must learn to focus on feeling rather than thinking, when they are actually practising.

I have often asked pupils to make a descent and then describe what they experienced – or were *aware of.* Too often the answer comes back in thinking terms and not awareness terms.

For example: 'I didn't go up and down enough.' 'How do you know that? What did you actually *feel* that told you that?' 'I felt my legs bent all the time, crouching and tight as I turned.'

'Good! *That* is the experience. *That* is what you *were* aware of, the rest was only thinking.'

Awareness is experiencing directly, thinking is conceptualizing about experience. They are different processes and there is reason to believe that as thinking increases, so awareness decreases simultaneously.

The time for thinking is between practices, but during practice *Awareness* is vital if the pupil is going to develop and improve.

Vision locates obstacles and pathways, and gives a reference for balance.

Touch and Hearing give information about the nature of the surface being skied upon, and of changes in it. These senses also give information which indicates the speed of travel. Whenever possible, guidance should be given to the pupil to help him to use these senses more efficiently. The instructor should be able to translate mechanical information into physical terms and help the pupil to sharpen his senses by pinpointing the key factors.

For example: what to look and listen for in the timing of movements, and what to feel for in the application of weight or pressures within the body shape. The importance of these perceptual skills can be illustrated by a conversation between two skiers about to set off down Corrie Cas (a run on Cairngorm) in a complete 'white out'. One skier, having considerable problems of balance and control, asked the other, a well-known director of a local ski school, how he managed to ski at all when he could not even see the snow underneath his skis because of the mist and flat lighting. The ski school director replied with words to the following effect, 'Skiing is like flying by the seat of your pants! Use the soles of your feet, laddie, they'll tell you what's going on down there!'

Finally, the instructor should be aware that beginners, especially youngsters, often appreciate an opportunity to have their newly-acquired skills tested. A simple slalom on an open or handicapped basis will often suffice, though the imaginative instructor will be able to improvise and produce a 'game' which will appeal to all his students, regardless of their ability. He must remember also that, in the words of Sir Arnold Lunn, 'The purpose of skiing is to increase the sum total of fun.'

The ability of an instructor to develop a student's skill through and beyond the basic swing turn is related to his understanding of the fundamental techniques and how they fit into the overall scheme of things. It is dependent on his understanding of the workings of the human body, from physical and psychological points of view, and on his appreciation of the more advanced aspects of skilful skiing.

The instructor should always strive to increase his knowledge and his personal performance through reading, discussion and constant practice, and by attending as many ski instructors' training courses as he can.

Information about such courses can be obtained from the Secretary or Coaches of the Regional Ski Federations, or from the Secretary of the English Ski Council, or the Secretary of the British Association of Ski Instructors.

Instruction Procedure Summary

Before you begin any period of instruction you should ask yourself *three* questions:

(1) What, precisely, am I trying to teach?

    e.g. developing sliding, balance or steering.

(2) How will I know when I have taught it?

    ... revise it at frequent intervals, and set 'task' exercises to assess the level of the students' skill.

(3) Am I giving the student as much help as I possibly can?

    e.g. (a) Choice of suitable exercises.

        (b) Choice of suitable terrain.

        (c) Suitability of student's equipment.

        (d) *Always progress from known to unknown.*

In respect of question (3), bear in mind the following points:

1. Students will learn well only if they are safe and comfortable.
2. Students will learn well only if they are enjoying themselves.
3. ... if they are making progress (related to 3a above).

    The instructor's praise *of successful attempts*, and personal interest, will be a major factor in determining pupils' progress.

(4) Do not criticize unnecessarily. Give positive directions at the next attempt (e.g. do not say 'Your weight is on your heels, don't sit back', but something like 'Feel yourself standing on the balls of your feet').

Give Direction and Encouragement

(5) Remember, students only learn by doing. Do not talk too much and confuse them with unnecessary technicalities. Give them maximum activity, and encourage maximum awareness.

Practice not Preaching

Fault Detection

It is impossible to describe every possible fault, but there is a basic procedure for detecting and dealing with faults:

Detecting faults:

Look for the major faults first. In steering, edge control, pressure control!

(a)   Does the student have a good, loose, balanced posture?

(b)   Is he standing on his feet correctly?

(c)   Is he clear in his mind what it is he is trying to do?

(d)   Is he afraid of speed, steepness, exposure? Is he tense or nervous?

(e)   Does he start the manoeuvre in complete control of himself?

(f)   Is he pushing/pressing against his feet correctly?

(g)   Does he have any upper body mannerisms which hinder his leg work?

Correcting the faults:

(a)   Work on one fault at a time.

(b)   Try to correct with verbal instruction while practising (e.g. try to describe the correct feeling of the action, or command positively).

(c)   It is possible that as awareness of a fault increases (perhaps through concentration during positive practice of that fault) the pupil will correct or improve himself dramatically as realization of what is actually happening dawns on him. Increase awareness.

(d)   You may need to isolate the fault; give a demonstration of it.

(e)   Resort to practising at a standstill, or in 'non-gravity' situations, only if (a) to (d) fail.

(f)   Revert to earlier practices.

APPENDIX B

A Specimen Lesson on an Artificial Slope

Class   Nine adults (beginners).
        One person is rather heavy and awkward in his movements, everyone else appears quite agile.
Period $1\frac{1}{2}$ hours.
Slope   Artificial 40 ft wide × 40 ft long and the flat run out measures 40 ft × 20 ft.

A Suggested Outline of Procedure for the Instructor.

Introduce yourself to the class and try to learn all their names. Take the class to the flat area at the bottom of the slope and, with everyone facing the same way, ask them to put on their equipment. Ask each person to twist his toe irons to both sides to see that they are operational. The toe pieces should be set very lightly for this lesson. As the pupils put on their skis, you may have to help one or two. Ask them to take them off and put them on again. Time spent now in learning this will save a lot of bother on the slope later. You put on your skis.   *5 minutes*

Spread everyone out on the flat area so there is adequate space surrounding each student. Some exercises from *Groups Two* and *Four* can now be used to accustom the students to their 'new selves' and so that they can recognize the size and awkwardness of their equipment. Some exercises from *Groups One* and *Four* can also be done to warm up. If the weather is particularly cold, some warming-up exercises could be done before the skis are put on.   *5 minutes*

Keep the Class Warm and Moving

Teach star/clock turns.

Demonstrate the action of walking and ask everyone to attempt it. Organize a route which goes a little way onto the slope, and ask the class to form a line and follow the route, turning and avoiding obstacles as they go. Watch for rhythmic, loose, well coordinated movements, especially in the legs.

The awkwardness of the slower student begins to show itself now; put him at the end of the line so that he does not hold the others up, but encourage him so that he does not feel left behind.   *10 minutes*

Arrange games, relay races, etc., to add some degree of competition to increase interest and to test their new abilities. Put yourself in the same team as the weak student to even things up. He must not feel that he is holding his team up too much.   *10 minutes*

Line up the class in ranks of three on the flat run out, facing across the slope. Explain the upper and lower ski and fall line. Teach side-stepping exercises, sideways running, etc.

Face the class during introductory explanations, but demonstrate facing in the same direction as the class, so that they can identify easily with you. The students should learn all manoeuvres to both sides, but when introducing them to new ones, consider the direction of the wind and the sun, as it is not easy to concentrate with the sun or wind in your face.

Extend the side-stepping from the flat onto the slope; side-shuffle down. Draw attention to the sound of shuffling and brushing the edges.

It now becomes clear that one of the students has skied before, probably about a week or so. For personal reasons she wanted to start again from the beginning.

There is a tendency for this student to stand too much on the sides of her feet. Discourage this and show her the way of standing on the balls of the feet. In any event, she is obviously the strongest student in the group. Use this student to help you lead the class. She leads the class up one side of the mat, across the slope and shuffles down the other side, following the rectangular track. You can devote your time to helping the weaker students. Practise to both sides.   *approximately 15 minutes*

On the flat, teach star/clock turns with stick support.

Divide the class into two ranks, facing each other from each side of the slope. The strong student can lead one side while you lead the other, up the slope to a height which will give you a slow schuss.

You move out and demonstrate the star turns into the fall line with stick support and then basic schuss.

Everyone should attempt this, schussing down the slope two at a time. Make sure each student uses both sides of the slope. Teach schussing until the end of the period. (Make schusses progressively longer.)

As the slope is wide enough, allow the students to climb up and ski down at their own rate. (Not necessarily in one line or two, one or two at a time.)

Make sure the run out is clear before setting off.

End of Period

Make a note of the pupils' names and what they have learned. This will enable you to continue their instruction without confusion during their next period. (They may not come until the next week, and you may have many classes before then and have difficulty remembering what you taught.) Now that you know what their abilities are, you might consider preparing a lesson plan for their next session. Write down your aim and some possible exercises, along with any coaching points you consider relevant to them.

A lesson plan will help you to give a balanced and well-timed lesson with complete confidence.

Specimen Lesson Plan

Class   Nine beginners who have had one lesson.
One person is heavy and awkward, and one other has skied for a week before.

Time $1\frac{1}{2}$ hours.

Aim   To improve balance and to introduce side-skiing and snowploughing.

Introduction

Running around on the flat, forwards, backwards and sideways.

Recap schussing and step-turning on the slope.

Main Theme	Coaching Points
1. Recap side-shuffling.	Forward ankle bending.
2. Attempt to side-skid.	Easy shuffling movement, tilt upper body downhill. Hips face downhill slightly.
3. Practise to both sides.	
4. Recap gentle schussing.	
5. Introduce snowplough.	1. Skis in 'V' shape – stiff, straight legs.
	2. Kneel forwards towards tips of skis. (Bow-legged people kneel slightly inwards, knock-kneed people kneel directly forwards.)
	3. Lower hips slightly.
	4. 'Sag', relax and let weight hold skis in position.
6. Plough, running to a halt on flat.	
7. Plough, schuss on the run out.	
8. Plough, bending and straightening at knees and ankles.	Loose, rhythmical movements, 'feeling' in feet for skidding against the edges.
9. Supervised free practice.	

Teaching Young Children to Ski

Children should never be persuaded to learn to ski against their will. A child who skis entirely to please his parents or teacher is likely to give it up at the first opportunity.

Whenever possible, children should learn to ski in small groups. It does no good to children or adults if they are mixed in the same class, unless the children are very young (seven and under) and then the parents could accompany them, unless the class is catering specially for young children – then it is best if the parents are not present.

The age that a child should be introduced to skiing depends entirely on the child – his strength, physical condition, and his enthusiasm to ski. Generally speaking, seven is a suitable age to learn to ski on an artificial slope, whereas under suitable conditions, a child of four or five will take to skiing on the snow. Children at this age learn to ski exclusively for their own pleasure. Comfort is essential. After seven, the presence of the parent becomes less desirable, as the child tends to respond better when he is alone or with other children.

Equipment

The child should be well protected from the weather, the snow and/or the artificial slope. Adequate strong warm clothing is required and waterproof trousers or one piece suits are ideal for the snow. Mitts and hats should always be worn, sun cream and goggles are essential to protect skin and eyes from the strong reflected light of the snow.

Skis   These should be lightweight, have a good running surface and intact edges. The length is not important, but they should not be any longer than shoulder height.

Bindings It is often said that children do not require release bindings, as their bones are not as brittle as adults. This may be so, but their muscles are not as developed as adults' and their slight weight demands great efficiency from a release binding, to ensure adequate protection of their joints and bones. Release bindings are made with special release tensions for children.

Sticks   Children like to use equipment which is the same as the adults' equipment. Sticks are no exception. They should have handles, straps, baskets and *rounded* points. They should be lightweight and about waist high. Tonkin cane sticks should be avoided. These splinter if they break.

Boots The boots must keep the feet warm and dry. They must be very comfortable or the child will, quite rightly, refuse to wear them. (Incidentally, there is no reason for boots to be uncomfortable for anyone, children or adults.) They should give adequate lateral support to the ankle, without interfering with the forward bending action. Young children often ski with rigid ankles, but this must not be aggravated by the boot.

Children do not respond favourably to over-formal instruction, which adults will accept. They know instinctively that they will 'learn by doing'. Games must be organized which will present them with specific problems and the instructor should guide them and act more like a referee and team manager than a demonstrating lecturer.

When given, demonstrations must be first class: children are adept imitators. After imitating a correctly demonstrated posture or movement, they can then learn to cope with simple problems. Do not interfere with this process by giving excessive explanations.

1. Create the learning situation, set them a problem or challenge.
2. Indicate possible path of action.
3. Command action, 'Get going'.
4. Alter learning situation to correct faults. Do not ask a child to repeat his first attempts (which he felt to be successful) once you have corrected him. Praise his efforts, and alter the task you set.
5. Encourage safe, free practice. 'Practice makes perfect' may not always be true, but practice certainly improves!

The result of children's learning is different from that of adults. Adults' progress is quite rapid initially and then settles down to a steady improvement, whereas children tend to take considerably longer to find their feet, but once they gain confidence, they will soon become more accomplished than the majority of adults.

Patience and perseverance from the instructor over this initial period will be well rewarded by later results and the enthusiasm and joy which accompany them.

Use of an easy ski tow should be attempted as soon as possible. Children are interested in 'skiing', not in learning techniques, and using a gentle ski tow will increase their enthusiasm and speed the learning process.

By using a ski tow on a gentle slope, children will soon learn basic swing turns. They will not need as much isolated practice in side-slipping as adults, and will simply 'skid around corners' when the occasion demands, if they are given sufficient free running and plough/turning practice.

'What is true for children is probably true for adults too.' (Horst Abrahams, Interski Address, Zao, January 1979.)

EXERCISE PLAN

Descriptions of exercises which can be used to develop the fundamental techniques of skiing. The plan includes instructional notes which indicate the important aspects of the movements to be emphasized when the exercises are being practised.

Exercise	Description
Warming up and equipment familiarization exercises	See Chapter Two, *Pre-Ski Training.* These exercises should be practised on level ground.
Walking on the level	This differs from ordinary walking only because the feet are slid forward and not lifted. The arms, via the sticks, are used for propulsion. When practised vigorously the gliding step emerges. (See illustration 33.)
Turning on the level	While walking forward, the student lifts one ski at an angle to his direction of travel. The other ski is brought alongside. This process is continued until the new direction is achieved.
Star turn or clock turn	Turning when stationary. Step the skis round like the arms of a clock, i.e. around a circle whose centre is the tips or heels of the skis (a combination of the above uses less space).
Side-stepping	Standing across the fall line, the pupil should get the feel of his edges by standing with his feet a little apart and the 'upper' foot slightly advanced. He then kneels and pushes firmly against the 'big toe' of the lower foot. The angle of push can be varied so that the ski is pushed sideways over the surface, or only downwards into the surface. By this kneeling and pressing, the ski can be controlled so that the student can push himself sideways in an active but otherwise side-stepping manner.

Notes regarding quality execution to be emphasized by the ski instructor

The movement should be very free and easy, with loose, not awkward leg movements. Discourage any lifting of the skis.

The student should lift the knee in order to lift the ski, and not lift the leg stiffly from the hip.

The student should be encouraged to move on the balls of the feet, to prevent awkward movement now and later on.

This should be practised on the flat, until eventually the student will be able to 'run' sideways. Care must be taken to 'bend the ankle' prior to the push of the lower foot.

Side-stepping is taught in this way to prevent the student from learning to stand on the sides of his feet (which so often happens) preventing mobility and producing awkward body posture.

Herringboning

Starting from a 'V' stance, step forward, maintaining an angle of about 30°–45° between the skis. Pressure is applied against the inside edges of the skis.

Side-stepping down 'shuffling'

This is the ideal opportunity for the student to learn basic control over the sideways movement of the skis. He should keep the skis on the plastic/snow *at all times.* He kneels and pushes the lower ski sideways as in above exercise (against the inside of the ski; on the snow this will move the top layer of snow). The upper ski is brought to the lower by pulling against the outer edge (little toe). Small 'shuffling' steps should be made without lifting either ski, and as confidence develops so may a slight side-skid. (See illustration 45.)

45.   *Karina Zarod side-stepping*

Turning on the slope

Standing across the fall line, the student reaches downhill with both ski sticks. The tips should be placed downhill of the student's feet and ski tips. With arms as straight as possible and hands on the top of the sticks, the student supports his

On small slopes, herringboning takes up too much space to be useful at this stage. When it is taught, 'kneel forwards and inwards' is a useful command.

The command is 'kneel, push, kneel, pull'. The lower leg must remain bent, as the upper one is pulled down. The student must not be allowed to lift his feet, as it will cause stiff ankles. He should keep 'kneeling down' throughout the whole movement. He is, in fact, learning incidentally to steer his skis, and is preparing to learn the steering of the inner ski which will be necessary for one form of basic swing turn.

As in all techniques where the skis are across the fall line (side-skidding, traversing, etc.), the student's hips must tend to face downhill; on no account must they face uphill. Prevention now will reduce the need for cure later.

This can be rehearsed beforehand on the flat. A common fault here is that the student allows his feet to come too far downhill when he can no longer support himself. 'Step backwards uphill as you step around' is a useful phrase. The weight of the student should be carried mainly on the balls of his feet.

weight thus while he steps around into the fall line. To commence the downhill run the student should stand erect, and then push the sticks forward, thus releasing himself, and pick them up as he goes past. (See illustration 46.)

N.B. The descriptions of 'side-stepping' up and down given here are as comprehensive as possible, because this stage of a pupil's learning is most important if he is to develop a sound basic posture. The problems of side-stepping are often magnified by small artificial slopes with steep gradients. The time spent instructing these techniques need not be great, however, and teaching methods should not be involved and technical. Clear demonstrations, with key points of the movements emphasized, should suffice.

Basic schussing

The basic schuss is the student's first experience of a sliding situation. His future development is dependent on the way in which he copes with schussing. He should maintain balance, cope with acceleration and deceleration, and should control the direction of travel of his skis and not merely keep up with them. His general posture should be erect, ankles and knees bent (neither fully so) and the weight of his body carried over the whole of both feet, these being hip-width apart. His hands should hold the sticks firmly, and should be held about hip height, forward and to the side of him. The head should be held up and facing the direction of travel. (See illustration 47.)

Exercises to develop schussing ability

1. Attempt a schuss.
2. As above, with knee and ankle bending and straightening.
3. Schuss, pushing knees and hips forward and down.
4. High stretching and low crouching. (To touch and avoid obstacles, perhaps the instructor's sticks).
5. Touch bindings and return to basic posture.
6. Without sticks, picking up objects previously

This is an appropriate time to draw students' attention to the sound of the skis on the slope. Increased awareness of the sounds and feelings of skiing can improve learning rapidly.

46.   *'Turning on the slope' with stick support*

'Slope shyness' and unfamiliarity with the equipment will tend to produce defensive posture, i.e. insignificant ankle bend and stiff joints, too much knee and hip bending and general crouching.

Before further progress is attempted, exercises should be used to develop a comfortable, relaxed schuss, and to eliminate stiffness and defensive postures in the student. Any stiffness or awkwardness of movement remaining will be retained as the student progresses.

The ideal terrain for introducing the basic schuss is a very gentle slope, with adequate flat run out and slight counterslope. The importance of the terrain cannot be overstressed. At this stage the student should not need to know how to stop under his own power, otherwise 'slope shyness' will be reinforced and an efficient posture will not develop.

Look for easy movements in the ankle joints.

laid alongside track, i.e. sponge, hat, glove, etc.

7. Sliding feet forward alternately.
8. Turning head around, without allowing this to affect direction of travel of skis.
9. Turning upper body as above.
10. Two students side by side, passing small objects, one to another.
11. Lifting heels alternately.

12. Rapid extending of the legs from a slight crouch to unweight the skis (gentle hopping).
13. Schussing. Step feet together, apart, together, apart.
14. Stepping, skis parallel to left/right.
15. Stepping out of direction of schuss, initially of the run out; when successful on the slope itself.
16. Schussing over bumps and hollows. The head (and centre of gravity) should tend to remain level, as the legs bend and straighten.

Students may choose their own exercises and thereby increase their involvement and concentration, especially if their exercises must be different from (say) the adjacent classmate's.

This approach also ensures that each student has the *least* probability of failure. Reinforce his efforts and encourage sound development of them.

The student must 'stand down' on the ball of the foot.

47. *Basic schuss*

Care must be taken here to ensure that the pupil extends his legs and does not pull his feet up under him.

Ensure that the pupil steps off the ball of the foot, not the heel. 'Push off the right/left big toe!'

Build these with a shovel if no natural ones are to be found. On artificial slopes, these can be portable. If the slope is wide enough, as many pupils as is safe should practise together, once they are able to descend the slope with some stability. Ensure a clear run out before starting.

Falling

The pupil should try to recognize when he is losing control and falling, and not fight it but to keep tight hold of his sticks, keep his hands in front of him and sit down to the side of his skis (uphill if he is not in the fall line). He should *extend his legs* as he sits down and lie flat on his *back.* (See illustration 48.)

48.   *When falling extend the legs*

Standing again

The student should uncross his legs, free his arms and sticks and get his skis together, facing the same way.
1. If on a slope, skis downhill and across the fall line.
2. Sitting as close to the skis as possible, he should place one hand on the slope, as near to the upper thigh as possible, and then push up off that hand, simultaneously straightening the legs, keeping the upper body forward. (See illustration 50.)

50.   *Colin Whiteside shows how to stand again*

Keeping hold of the sticks will prevent injury to fingers, especially on artificial slopes. He should lie on his back, because the initial bounce may cause him to twist a knee or injure the lower leg if the upper body tends to overtake the skis and the knee has dug into the slope and stopped.

Momentum will cause the body to continue past the knee.

49.   *If the knee digs in, momentum can cause a twisted knee or worse*

If snow is soft, assistance from the sticks may be needed.

N.B. The instructor may consider it useful to instruct students in how to fall, even before they attempt to schuss. In any event, instruction in falling should be given during the first session.

The student's overall objective is now to make *rhythmically linked skidded turns* on very easy terrain. To enable him to achieve this aim, he must learn various techniques which will allow him to gain control over himself and his skis in various sliding situations. These techniques are indicated on the teaching plan. The order of learning is not mandatory but it must be borne in mind that what is learned first determines how and what is learned later. To this end the following points are worth noting.

1. Movements to control the side-skidding of the skis under the influence of *momentum* should be introduced as soon as possible – in addition to, but distinct from, side-slipping where *gravity* is the sole directional motive force.
2. Ploughing should be taught to aid steering and turning, and not encouraged for braking.
3. These techniques should be learned in such a way as to contribute to the basic swing turning, without alteration.

Side-slipping

Assume the same basic posture as for side-stepping but with a slight forward bend at the hips and with the head over the lower foot. Hands low but held forward of the body.

Instructional Note On most artificial ski slopes, side-slipping can be introduced at this stage as a logical sequence to 'side-shuffling' down as indicated in exercise 1 below.

To side-slip effectively, under the direct influence of *gravity* alone, the skis should be maintained approximately at right angles to the fall line. The degree of 'edge' must be less than that which would hold the skis still on the same slope. Side-slipping is, therefore, permitted by *releasing the grip* of the edges and allowing the skis to slip downwards. A good 'angulated' posture is essential if side-slipping is to be controlled efficiently and effectively.

1. As exercise above, 'side-stepping down, shuffling'. The upper body tends to lead the movement, thus enabling a smooth slipping to continue after the shuffling has started the movement.
2. The student should assume the general side-skidding posture and push himself downhill with his sticks.

N.B. On suitable gentle snow slopes, plough-gliding steering will enable
     students to use ski tows at an early stage, thus accelerating their
     learning.

Beginners should not be asked to ski down a slope that they have not
previously walked up.
   The most suitable terrain to learn side-slipping and traversing on should
be steeper than that used for basic schussing and ploughing. Learning to
side-slip on too flat terrain can encourage habits which interfere with the
execution of efficient swing turns.

   Side-slipping is used for:
(a) increasing awareness of the sideways movement of the skis.
(b) losing height on steep or awkward terrain.

These exercises should be used until the pupil can initiate a controlled
side-slip by sinking from a high stance, i.e. a relaxed kneeling action.

Do not allow lower leg to be pushed out straight, nor the weight to be
carried by the upper foot. 'Kneel down and resist slightly with the feet.'
The student must stand on the upper edges of the soles of the feet, with the

3. The student should assume the general side-skidding position, and hold the sticks at one end, while the instructor stands below, facing him, holding the other ends. The instructor pulls the student sideways, 'talking him down'. (See illustration 51.)

51. *Being pulled sideways enables the pupil to 'feel' the sideways movement of the skis*

4. Facing the direction of intended travel, but keeping the skis across the fall line, the student should 'hop' sideways downhill until the skis start to slip.

5. Facing slightly downhill of the ski tips, the student should stand erect on the heel of his upper foot. He should move the upper body forwards and downhill smoothly and as he feels his weight move onto the ball of the lower foot, he should bend the knees and ankles, and allow the skis to slip. (See illustration 52.)

ankles well bent; on no account must he be allowed to stand on the sides of his feet to 'edge' the skis.

52. *Side-slipping exercise: Karina angulates, and so moves off the heels and onto the balls of the feet. The upper body leads the movement*

The success of this exercise depends upon a good leg extension and a soft landing followed by a sinking-down at the ankles. The character of the movement must be light and easy. Control will be lost if the student lands on his heels.

The upper body should lead this movement. Emphasis on feeling for the weight transference will improve the execution of this exercise. The legs should not be bent stiffly as they begin to slip. The legs 'sag' at the ankles.

The knees but not the hips should move out from the hill to release the edges. 'Angulation' of the upper body enables balance to be maintained when the skis begin to slip.

Diagonal side-
slipping

The direction of the side-slip will depend on where the skis are weighted in relation to the amount of side resistance. Generally, weight forward will indicate a forward side-slip, weight back, a backward side-slip.

Ploughing

At the feet, the action of ploughing is the same as side-skidding. The general posture of the body while ploughing is the same as that in the basic schuss, except that the feet are wider apart and the legs are rotated slightly inwards. Due to the distance between the feet, the body-weight is carried on the inner part of the soles of the feet and through to the inner edges of the skis.

53.   *Basic snowplough*

To control the slip regardless of direction, the ankles should remain bent. The forward or backward transfer of weight from centre initiates the change in direction of travel. When in motion one's weight should be centralized above the whole of the feet again.

The 'snow plough' is ideal for teaching 'turning by leg action'. It also allows the pupil to develop more confidence in the control of his feet when side-skidding. This technique should always be comfortable to the pupil, never awkward. No isolated edging of the skis by the feet alone should be permitted. The angle of the skis is maintained purely by the efficient application of body weight.

'Learning' plough   Support in the fall line as for a basic schuss. Step
                           skis out into a 'V' between 30° and 40°. Stand
                           perpendicular to the slope with stiff, straight legs.
                           Kneel forwards *towards* tips of skis.
                           Lower hips and relax.
                           Let weight hold skis in position.

Gliding plough   The plough angle is narrow, and the breaking
                           effect is insignificant. (See illustrations 54 and
                           55.)

54 and **55.**   *Two views of a refined, gliding snowplough*

This is to set skis on the correct, symmetrical 'edge'.

If skier is bow-legged, kneel inwards, if knock-kneed, kneel directly forwards. Remove sticks and plough down the fall line.

This technique should be developed to help the student to turn.

55.

Breaking plough   The hips are lowered, and the heels of the skis are pushed wide apart. The skis correspondingly become more edged. The breaking effect can be considerable at slow speeds. (See illustration 56.)

Exercises to improve control of ploughing action related to swing turns.

1. Maintain constant plough angle; rhythmically bend and straighten ankles and knees.
2. 'Bouncing' in ankles and knees will cause a widening and narrowing of the plough angle.
3. Attempt to maintain constant plough angle with very bent and then very straight legs.
4. Turn skis from almost parallel schuss into plough, and vice versa.
5. Keeping angle of plough constant, spread feet wide apart by straightening the legs; allow skis to run closer together again by bending the legs. Keep hips at a constant height above the slope throughout the total manoeuvre.

Instructional Note   The student's ability to control himself increases with every exercise. Do not allow the ploughing action to become too dominant at this stage. Recap side-slipping with skis parallel (not together) and schussing. If it is possible the student should practise what he has learned so far, during runs down gentle slopes served by a suitable ski lift.

The importance of this technique, as an aid to developing swing turns and dynamic skiing, is nil. Students will themselves realize the control which can be effected by ploughing, but they should not be encouraged to develop the use of the plough for breaking in the fall line. All further mention of ploughing will refer to gliding ploughing, unless otherwise stated.

56. *Braking snowplough*

Terrain as for basic schussing.

The spreading of the feet must be accompanied by a slight bending of the ankles.

Students must avoid bending forward from the waist and stiffening the legs.

The student learns to plough with his feet and not with a total body action. In this way he can steer his skis more positively.

During these exercises, the student should develop enough control of himself to be able to plough from a schuss either by bending or straightening the legs, once the initial turning of the feet has been started (i.e. with the ankles slightly bent and the weight on the balls of the feet).

Traversing

When the control exerted on the skis during a side-skid is increased, the sideways movement of the skis can be prevented. The student can descend the slope at any angle to the fall line that he chooses. The skis will run forward in the direction they are pointing without any sideways slipping occurring. The movements necessary to control the slip will vary just as the angle of descent varies. Therefore, the difference between the body shape in a basic schuss and in a traverse will increase as the angle between the fall line and traverse increases.

57. *Neil Shepperd, England Team member, demonstrates a traverse*

Exercises to develop traverse

1. During a side-slip, incline upper body downhill and at the same time kneel and press 'big toe' of lower foot firmly into snow/mat. If the skis are pointing downhill at all, they will now run along their edges. Traverse.
2. Attempt traverse of slope.
3. As above, ankle and knee bending and straightening.
4. Attempt to 'jet' the feet forward. That is, project them along the track with a rapid 'flick' from the knees.
5. Lift upper ski.

The resistance to sideways movement must be increased very vigorously. Once the traverse has been achieved, the resistance can be reduced because the effort required to stop the slipping is greater than the effort needed to hold the traverse.

The student must grip by correct application of weight to the feet. He must not stand on the side of his feet. In this respect, an isolated lateral movement of knees to edge the skis must be strongly discouraged, as must an isolated sideways movement of the ankles.
The knees must be pressed forward. (See illustration 57.)

6. Lift lower ski.
7. Turn upper body.
8. Extend lower arm and stick as far as possible downhill, keep basket on slope, approximately level with heels of skis.
9. Gentle springing to produce unweighting.
10. Traverse, pull the upper ski down to the lower ski, against its upper edge (little toe). Lift out again to wide stance.
11. With skis together, traverse, step up into a higher parallel track.
12. Step up into a shallower traverse.

Recap ploughing

Recap ploughing exercises with emphasis on leg action.

Plough turning

1. While moving downhill in a gliding plough, the student repeatedly pushes out against one ski.
2. Repeat with other ski, then alternate skis.

58. *Faults which can develop in snowplough turns (see 54 above) will cause problems later as in this skier's attempts to skid with parallel skis*

The correct posture will only be achieved if the palm is turned upwards.

If the student lands softly with relaxed ankles, a tendency to side-slip should occur.
Bend in knees and ankles should *increase* as feet come together.

Each step must be made by pushing off the ball of the lower foot, and not by lifting body-weight by straightening of the upper leg.

The ski must be pushed *backwards* not forwards. The tip of the weighted ski must be behind the tip of the other one.

3. Attempts to steer the skis should be made, with the legs only slightly bent. The turning is achieved by increase of pressure against the big toes.

59. *Linked snowplough turns.*
Note: slight but accurate angulation keeps head over the 'big toe' of the steered ski

If necessary, exaggerated knee pressure against 'big toe' must be made to prevent a tendency to turn by stiffening legs and twisting hips. A good posture and efficient turning of the legs but *not* the hips must develop at this stage if problems are to be avoided later. (See illustration 59.) To aid anguiation, put the head above the 'big toe' of the steering (outer) foot.

4. Continuous linked turns.

Technical Note Snowplough and snowplough turns are aids to learning basic swing turning. Therefore, the snowplough and snowplough turns should not be skied any longer than absolutely necessary. As soon as possible, the turning of the inside ski should be attempted. This may emerge on gentle runs serviced by a suitable ski lift.

Plough Swing

1. Recap Direct Ploughing
2. From a fall line plough, reach well forward with hands and bend forward at hips. *Very quickly* move one ski parallel to the other. Keep weight on balls of feet. A diagonal side-skid will result.
3. When 2 above is achieved consistently, the student should kneel down during the skid phase.
4. If anxiety in a student is too high, these exercises may be attempted from a traverse but in this case, care must be taken to ensure that the lower ski is skidding sideways when the upper is turned parallel to it.

Technical Note Side-skidding can appear as similar to side-slipping, but there is a fundamental difference of which the instructor must be aware if safe and useful 'skidded' turns are to develop.

Side-slipping is initiated by a release of the skis' edges, permitting gravity to pull the skis (and skier) sideways. During the initiation phase, the skis are flattened towards the slope (slightly).

Side-skidding is initiated by turning (or standing onto a ski already turned, as in the plough) an appropriately edged ski, across the direction of momentum of the skier.

N.B. Side-slipping is started most easily on a steep hillside, when the skier is stationary and his skis are horizontal.

Side-skidding can be performed on flat ground, with momentum, and cannot be started from a stationary, horizontal position, but rather is most easily achieved from a descent close to the fall.

The two techniques are least distinguishable at

'Steer the feet'. Upper body must be very loose and return to middle position before the next turn across the fall line.

Ensure that student has a good upright posture, legs nearly straight, hands well forward. By stabilizing the upper body, bent forward and arms forward and out (the moment of inertia is increased around the longitudinal axis), the ski which is *preventing* turning is *removed* and provided that no disturbance is made to the other ski it will continue to skid, under the momentum gained in the plough.

Good hip and knee angulation during the parallel skid phase will permit greater control of the speed and direction of the skid. Students should be encouraged to lift the 'inner' ski by bending the knee and hip, but to do so quickly and place parallel to the skidding ski as soon as possible.

60. *Plough swing*

moderate speed on medium traverse lines, but the instructor must differentiate the characteristics of both and be in no doubt that it is side-skidding not side-slipping which forms part of skiing turns. Indeed, attempts by students to side-slip during a turn will invariably result in a fall outwards due to 'catching an outside edge'.

Steering the inner ski   When a simple plough swing has been achieved consistently by 'removing' the inner ski, this ski can now be used actively to reinforce the work of the outer ski. Instead of being lifted, it should remain on the surface but change edge (from inner to outer) and turn across the direction of momentum until it is parallel to the outer ski.
1. Practise the movement at a standstill.

61. *Side-skidding – here shown from a traverse*
Note: skis are turned across *the direction of the skier's momentum*

62. *Steering the inner ski. Practice at a standstill*

2. Stand across the slope, feet in a narrow plough. Roll upper knee outwards and pull ski down on its 'little toe', outside edge.
3. Plough across the slope, ensuring lower ski is skidding.
4. Initiate a skid by exercise 2 above.
5. Practice to both sides, at various speeds and angles of descent.
6. If pupils are adept at plough swing with lifting but have difficulty steering the inner ski parallel, the following exercise will probably help.

1. Induce a forward diagonal side-skid (either from a plough as above, or 'shuffle' from a traverse). When stability is felt, settle on upper ski and lift the lower; keep skidding.

Plough Swing Garlands

The effectiveness of linking manoeuvres for getting the 'feel' of the movements is well known, but linking plough swings in a Garland manner is also useful for reducing timidity in pupils who have a high anxiety of crossing the fall line.

63. *Plough swing garlands*

1. From a traverse, feet about 12 inches apart, roll upper knee inwards and steer the ski, against the inside edge, causing a turn downhill.
Run out in a gliding plough onto a safe run out.

Keep both skis on the slope throughout the movement.

Legs almost straight.

Bend both legs as skis become parallel.
Good angulated posture, hands well forward, with bend at hips, as skis are turned parallel.

The student must face slightly downhill of his skis, angulate at the hips and keep ankles well bent.

This 'stemming' action can be accompanied by a low posture for timid pupils but must be developed into a high posture, with extending legs, as soon as is practicable.

The pupil must steer but not try to brake in this exercise.

2. On successive attempts of the above exercise, a plough swing can be made from the fall line and these should be linked if the slope width permits.

Uphill swing.

1. From a steepish traverse, make a diagonal skid, with good angulation, increase edge resistance slowly and the skid will change direction, turning uphill.
2. From a steepish traverse, angulate slightly, bringing weight to bear upon the 'big toe' of the lower foot and then turn both feet to point slightly uphill maintaining, and then slightly increasing, the amount of edge.
3. The uphill swing can be considered to be the end of a plough swing and used as an exercise to this end, or it can be used as a means of coming to a halt.
   In order to stop quickly a powerful skid must be made, by turning the skis quickly and then edging firmly.

64. *Learning to steer the outer ski to begin a turn downhill*

In its simplest form an uphill swing is simply a curving sideskid. If the skid is initiated subtely and accurately, however, only the heels of the skis need skid a little sideways.

Good hip angulation is important if the legs are to be turned *without* any undesirable turning of the hips.

The resulting posture is known as 'angulation with anticipation' (the upper body continues to face the line of original momentum, thus it anticipates the next possible turn).

Basic Swing Turning   This is a means of linking together plough swings
                         and then refining and developing the movements
                         so that rhythmically linked basic parallel turning
                         emerges.
                         There is no single set form of Basic Swing as it
                         is a developing, evolving technique which
                         enables the student to attend to each and every
                         important element of linked parallel turning from
                         a stable and familiar base, without the refinement
                         of balance and timing which, when they develop,
                         will enable the parallel turns to emerge. If basic
                         swings are used for simply descending open
                         terrain, they may also be known as stem
                         christies. If, however, they are used, with
                         continual modification, to learn parallel skiing
                         their form must contain elements which are not
                         necessarily present in stem christies. These are:
                         1. Both skis must be weighted during the turns.
                            (Not always 50/50.)
                         2. Skis must be maintained at least at hip-width
                            apart.
                         3. Turns must be rhythmically linked.
                         4. In later stages of modification, weight is
                            transferred to the outer ski before it is steered
                            downhill.

65. *Basic swing turning*

1. Link plough swings.

2. Repeat, but ensure that the rising and sinking
   actions co-ordinate exactly with the steering
   and skidding phases.
3. Repeat. Emphasize the *rhythm* of the movements.
4. Repeat. Emphasize steering, not lifting of the
   inner ski.

High stance plough, extending the legs while steering downhill, sinking during the skid phase.

The extension of the legs should commence immediately the sinking is complete and the previous turn finished.

Use slalom poles, or better still, lines marked on the slope indicating a suitable pathway.

5. Repeat. Change emphasis during one descent from 4 above to 3 above.

N.B. With practice and confidence, students will be turning with only a very slight 'stemmed' phase. To develop completely parallel turns the following small modification is necessary:

6. As the student finishes one turn and starts the next, he should stand onto the upper ski and *not move the foot* (uphill) but *move the knee* (downhill).

   Roll from outer edge to inner edge of an already weighted ski and steer it against its edge into the turn.

7. Repeat descents of continuously linked swings. Attention to exercise 6 above, and an increase in tempo of the strong rhythmical movements, with accent on the extension and flexing of the legs, will enable basic parallel turns to emerge from the basic swing turns. As an alternative method to 'shuffling', a side-skid may be initiated by gently hopping sideways. It follows that a form of plough swing, and hence basic turn, can be developed from this movement.

Exercise to develop plough swing with hop

1. From increasingly steep traverses, spring gently to initiate the side-skid, and control the skid as in plough swing.

2. Plough in the fall line, and with rhythmic springing unweight the skis completely.

3. Repeat above, then hop *both* feet sideways; skid upon landing.

4. Traverse, stem out, and kneel down to plough to fall line. Plough in the fall line, repeat 4 above.

Swinging basic swing turns with hop

Traverse, stem out, plough to the fall line, spring lightly hopping *both* feet sideways. The inner ski will travel the most and change its edge; the outer ski will move only slightly sideways and will not change edge. Upon landing, a skid should occur which is controlled as in plough swing (above).

1. Students should descend slope making continuously linked basic swing turns.

Maintain forward pressure during initiation and skid phases of turn.

The student must stand up onto his outer foot, tilt himself downhill and turn both legs (downhill) simultaneously.

Immediately the knee begins to move downhill, the student will feel he is turning downhill.

Confidence and an 'attacking' attitude are necessary at this time.

Say 'Hop! hop! hop!'
The student must take off, and land, lightly on the balls of the feet.
Observe leg extension: the plough angle should be quite narrow.

The spring must be minimal, but sufficient to allow both feet just to leave the slope. The legs must extend fully, and the student must land on the balls of his feet.
The student should guard against 'turning' the body to help the skis turn. The change in direction will occur while the skis skid, and not while the skis are unweighted.

As confidence, coordination and fluency improve, the student will feel the stem phase is increasingly unnecessary and, indeed, inconvenient.

2. During a subsequent descent, the student will be able to dispense with the narrow plough or stem and simply hop on both skis, from one skid into another, turning to the other side.

As can now be seen, there are two forms of basic swing turn. The student traverses, stems the upper ski to make a plough towards the fall line, and then continues to turn across the fall line using the techniques learned in the plough swings.

N.B. These two forms of basic swing turning, although different, do complement each other. The form that is used most will depend upon the physical condition of the students and on the terrain. The former turn is most useful on long, gentle slopes for students who are not extremely athletic, heavy people and children. The second form of the turn is most useful on slightly steeper slopes, and can be used by very aggressive students to lead directly into short swings (parallel). Practice of the steered form of basic swing turn will greatly increase the student's ability to make precision turns, while practice of the second form of turn, with the hop, will increase his mobility and sense of rhythm for the turns. The rhythm of the turns can be further reinforced by the addition of a 'pole plant' in the basic swing turns with hop. The pole should be planted immediately prior to the hop. Both forms of basic swing turn will develop naturally into parallel turns, provided the vertical movements of the legs and the rhythm of the movements are maintained while the overall tempo is increased. The steered turns become pure parallel turns when the inner ski is turned and has its edges changed, simultaneously with the leg extension which turns the outside ski. The basic swings with hop become pure parallel turns when the student has reduced the plough phase of the movement to zero and can hop off both feet without ploughing first. This occurs naturally, provided the rhythm of the movements is maintained, i.e. continuous linked turns are practised, as opposed to individual turns performed in isolation.

The instructor who is familiar with traditional ski teaching systems will notice the omission of the stem turn and the stem christie. These are both valid turns in their own right and are used by skiers of all standards in open terrain. They have been omitted from this progression of exercises because they do not actively help the

An appreciation by the student that skidding is caused by hopping (in this case) the skis across the direction of his momentum at the beginning of the turn (the end of the previous one) will aid his accuracy.

The sinking down to control the skid now serves as a preparation to spring, for the initiation of the new turn.

Continuous turning should be encouraged. Slalom poles, etc., are useful here.

student to learn leg movement patterns which must be developed to master parallel skiing.

The student who learns to make basic parallel turns by this method has at his disposal the necessary techniques to be able to make stem christies if he should need to do so. An indication of progressions which can be learned from basic swing turning is given in the following diagram.

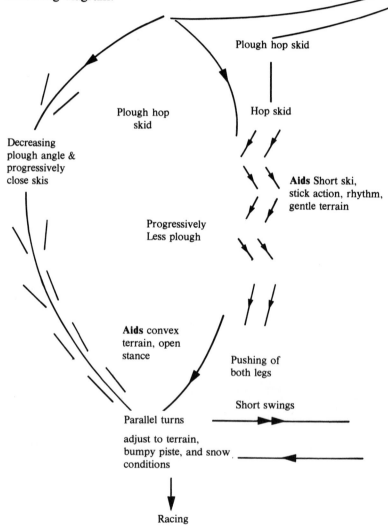

Plough hop skid

Plough hop skid

Hop skid

Decreasing plough angle & progressively close skis

Aids Short ski, stick action, rhythm, gentle terrain

Progressively Less plough

Aids convex terrain, open stance

Pushing of both legs

Short swings

Parallel turns

adjust to terrain, bumpy piste, and snow conditions

Racing

BASIC PROGRESSIONS

BASIC SWING TURNS

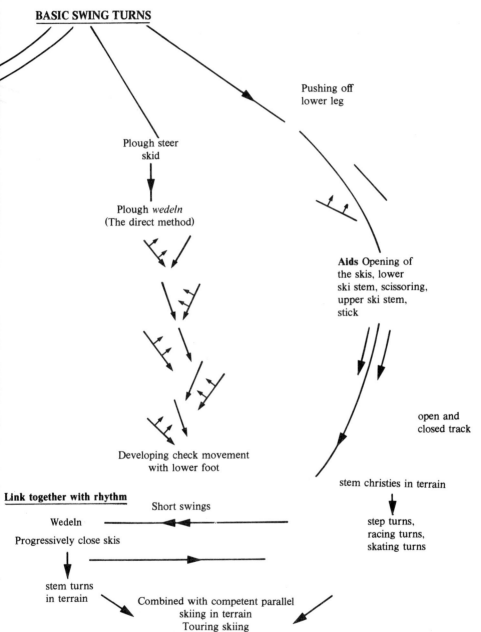

Pushing off
lower leg

Plough steer
skid

Plough *wedeln*
(The direct method)

Aids Opening of
the skis, lower
ski stem, scissoring,
upper ski stem,
stick

open and
closed track

Developing check movement
with lower foot

stem christies in terrain

Link together with rhythm

Short swings

Wedeln

step turns,
racing turns,
skating turns

Progressively close skis

stem turns
in terrain

Combined with competent parallel
skiing in terrain
Touring skiing

Parallel turns

There are many varied forms of parallel turns, all are identified by the simultaneous turning of both skis.

As parallel turns are subtle and usually performed at higher speeds than all other previously taught turns, they require good dynamic balance, characterized by an 'anticipating' attitude and balance, rather than by a 'responding' attitude and balance. Sensitive feet and good kinaesthesis are important at this stage if 'gross' basic movements are to be refined into efficient, skilful, parallel turning.

1. To improve dynamic 'anticipating' balance, at the end of one turn the body should be facing downhill, with the legs turned across the slope. ('Angulation with anticipation.') As the next turn commences, the skier should extend against the 'big toe' of the outer ski and, in addition, 'tilt' or 'dive' towards the centre of the anticipated turn. The stick may be planted to trigger off the extension and to provide some support during this movement.

2. The radius of a turn is determined by the degree of edging, speed and rotation of the legs.

Stick action

The ski sticks may be used for a variety of reasons: to push with or to assist in braking (in short swings) but they are used most often as an aid to timing.

1. The arm posture is vital if the sticks are to be used efficiently. Both hands should be carried forward off the body but with arms relatively straight (see illustrations).

2. The stick is planted to trigger the initiation of a turn. It is planted, therefore, at the very end of the sinking motion completing the skid phase, to trigger (and perhaps support) the initiation of the turn.

Technical Note Whenever continuously linked turns are made, the stick should be planted (for greatest mechanical effect) directly downhill of the feet, along a line 'drawn' from the supporting foot which indicates the instantaneous momentum of the skier.

66. *Basic parallel turn*

The direct method

This name is given to the method of learning parallel turns directly from snowploughing. It is most suitable on long, gentle, narrow slopes.
1. Link plough turns.
2. Accentuate the leg movements, bend to steer skis from fall line, extend to steer towards fall line.
3. Establish a sound rhythm, skiing close to the fall line.
4. Accentuate the change of weight from outer ski to outer ski.
5. Open ski tips during the sinking phase of the turn.
6. By increasing the tempo and maintaining a strong *rhythm* and sense of direction down the fall line, short radius parallel turns will begin to emerge, as movements become 'loose'. (See illustration 68).

Short swings

Short swings are a logical development of shortening the radius of parallel turns and provide good control on short, steep, sections of slope. (See illustrations 69 and 70.)
1. Using stick support, hop both ski heels from side to side.
2. Repeat above while moving slowly down on moderate slope. (Hand well forward, sticks pointing backwards.)
3. Plough *wedeln* with accentuated weight change and edge set.
4. Introduce sticks. Hands held forward, with the point being 'stabbed' to reinforce the edge set and trigger the hop.
5. Skilful short swings are characterized by a quiet landing, and a subsequent skid which is controlled by an appreciable, pronounced edge set, leading to a rebound, or spring. The legs turn independently; without hip rotation and with slight angulation the upper body faces and travels down the fall line continuously.

67. *The 'tilt' or movement of the hips downhill, towards the centre of the new turn, is illustrated by the Japanese demonstration team at Interski, Zao, Japan*

Emphasize steering action of outer ski.
Alternate between accentuating 'down, down, down', to 'up, up, up', on successive descents.

Keep hands forward and a quiet upper body, facing downhill. The legs turn independently underneath the torso!
Accuracy in pressure on the 'big toes' is vital here, the head must move above the ball of the (weighted) foot.
Turn the inside leg independently of the outer. Good angulation will prevent unwanted rotation of the hips.

Ensure extension of legs at take off, flexing on landing.
The landings must be 'quiet', each serving as the preparation for the subsequent take off.

69. *Basic short swings*
Note: independent but simultaneous rotation of the legs, in powerful extension and flexion

70. *Refined short swings*
Legs, though close together, turn independently. Upper body faces downhill while legs rotate with angulation

68. *The direct method*
Rhythmically linked plough turns, with powerful emphases on the vertical movements, can be developed into basic parallel, short radius turns

Before attempting to learn more advanced techniques, the student should become completely familiar with travelling downhill over varied, open terrain in a controlled manner.

Speed has a great influence on the execution of skiing techniques. The use of speed can only be learned by experience. Ground school techniques will help the student to experience speed on suitable terrain and to appreciate how it can be used to his advantage. Guidance from a qualified ski teacher is highly recommended while learning this.

When a student, who has completed a course of instruction on an artificial ski slope, goes to a ski instructor on the snow, he is invariably asked what he has accomplished. I would advise him, in his own interests, to be modest. He should say only how long (in days and hours) he has skied. He will then be given instruction which will be below his level of ability, but when he has adapted himself to the snow, he will progress to something commensurate with his true ability. There has come to my notice the instance of a student who had learned to make basic parallel turns on an artificial slope. When he arrived in the Alps, he told the ski school director, 'I can make parallel turns!' He was promptly allocated to a class and taken to the top of a cable car. The mere thought of what was expected of him set his nerves on edge! In this particular case, the ski school was at fault for not checking the student's ability before beginning the lessons, but in any case, it is always best to underestimate yourself on the first day of a skiing holiday. It is better for your morale to be the best skier in a class of near-beginners than to be the worst in a class of experts.

The most advanced skiing techniques can be learned much more easily if the basic training is good and reliable. Our Exercise Plan not only provides a training scheme for beginners who want to learn this most exhilarating and exciting sport, but it also forms a basis for the revision of fundamental techniques upon which skilful advanced skiing can be built.

A Glossary of Skiing Terms

Angulation

A dynamic balancing posture which enables refined edge control of skidded (and carved) turns. The upper body bends *forward* from the hips (its mass tending to follow its momentum), while the legs rotate to steer the skis.

Anticipation

The attitude of the skier which recognizes that the instantaneous momentum at the end of one turn will aid the initiation of the next.

The upper body, usually in angulation, faces the oncoming turn and during the initiation of that turn the upper body leads the movement.

Artificial Ski Slope

A surface other than snow which is used to ski upon. The majority of artificial ski slopes are made of monofilament PVC or injection-moulded plastics, though sand and silica waste from china-clay pits have been used.

Avalement

French word meaning 'swallowing'. It is used to describe a turning technique where the legs are rotated while bending and extending to keep a constant pressure between the soles of the skiis and the snow. The technique also uses leg movements which accelerate the skiis along the path of the turn. It is used most effectively on mogul piste and deep snow, and is characterized by pronounced knee bending for approximately half the turn.

Basic Swing Turning

Rhythmically linked turns, commencing with linked plough swings, which are continuously modified until parallel turns emerge.

A learning technique containing all the essential elements of parallel skiing but without the requirement of refined dynamic balance.

Carving   A technique for turning with maximum sliding (see skidding) and minimum braking of the skis. The ski runs along its own length, having been weighted, edged and deformed by this action into reverse camber which forms the arc of the turn. An efficient technique with minimum energy loss, used in racing.

71.   *Carving*
The ski, deformed into reverse camber, slides along an arced track

Christy also   See *Swing*.
Christiania

Counter Rotation   When the body is weightless or standing on a frictionless base, any attempt to turn one half of the body will result in the other half turning in the opposite direction. When a movement is made to turn the legs and skis into a turn while the skier is unweighted, the upper body will tend to turn and face outwards away from the turn. This effect is reduced, and the leg turning effect strengthened, if the upper body is 'fixed' by a firm planting of the ski stick. Counter rotation was a characteristic of turns made with poorer equipment than today and, therefore, skiers attempted to turn both legs as a single unit. The hips turned with the legs and the upper body counter-rotated. Today, it is a characteristic of poor technique which fails to use independent leg rotation.

Compression Turns   These turns, similar to *avalement* but without the active forward projection of the feet, are characterized by a folding of the legs (with rotation) to initiate the turn and an extension of the legs to complete the turn. Used on moguled or bumpy slopes to enable the skier to prevent 'terrain' unweighting.
Bend and turn, stretch and turn!

Edging   The lateral tilting of the skis towards the slope. Used to control the sideways movement of the skis.

Fall Line   That imaginary line which follows the steepest gradient of a slope.

GLM   Graduated Length Method. A method of teaching skiing using different lengths of skis. The beginner starts on very short skis and graduates to longer skis as his ability improves. In France a varient of GLM is known as *ski evolutif.*

Ground School   The basic school of skiing proposed initially by Karl Gamma of Interski in 1968, in Aspen. This part of the ski school would teach the fundamental techniques of skiing which would be the same in every country represented at the Interski congress. Now taken to mean the area of learning embracing fundamental skills of skiing.

Inner Ski   The ski which is nearer the centre of the turn.

Inner Skiing   An approach to learning skiing which accentuates the importance of awareness and experience, rather than instruction and thought in learning. It is a positive approach concentrating upon improving or changing what is being done, rather than dwelling on what could be, might be or should have been done.
Commercial, trans-national ski classes are being organized to teach this method.

72. *A compression turn*

Interski	An organization whose members are taken from the ski teachers' associations of each nation. The association meets at congresses held once every four years.
Method	See *Teaching Method.*
Moguls	Large rounded bumps in the ski slope, formed by the action of many skiers turning repeatedly in the same places in soft snow.
Motor Technique	Patterns of movement by parts, or the whole, of the body. See *Technique.*
Outer Ski	The ski which is further away from the centre of a turn.
Parallel Skiing	Skiing when the skis are kept parallel throughout the descent. Therefore, whenever the edges of the skis are changed, they are changed simultaneously.
Reciprocal Inervation	The reflex action which occurs in one set of muscles (*Antagonists*), causing them to relax so that they can lengthen when the opposite set of muscles (*Protagonists*) contract to produce power.

Release Bindings	The mechanisms which secure the skier's boots to his skis. They are designed to release the boots from the skis under certain pre-determined conditions of stress. The adjustments, which determine the point of release, must be made to the bindings in relation to the weight, strength, size (length of limb) and skill of the skier.
Reverse Shoulder	A technique used by many racers in the 1950s and 60s whereby the shoulders of the racer were turned away from the turn. This was done essentially to enable the racer to approach the slalom poles as closely as possible without hitting them with his shoulder. The movement also aided the turning of the whole lower body (see *Counter Rotation*), though in most cases this was not why it was used, as the skiers turned each leg independently from the hip socket, and not by turning the whole of the lower body, i.e. the legs and pelvis.
Schuss	Originally a German word meaning 'shot'. In skiing terms, it describes a run straight down the fall line.

Serpent Turn	Lined parallel turns, carved, with minimal side-skid and with constant ski-to-snow pressure throughout the turns.
Skilful Performance	A performance which realizes a goal, with minimum expenditure of time, effort or both, consistently and relating to the performers' limitations, e.g. age, strength, weight, sex, intelligence, etc.
Slalom Racing	Controlled downhill skiing between 'gates'. These are alternating pairs of red and blue flags. Giant slalom racing is a faster version of 'special' slalom; the gates are wider and further apart, though there are usually less of them, approximately 30–40 as opposed to 50–70 gates in 'special' slalom.
Skidding	A sideways movement of the skis, after they have been turned across the direction of *momentum* of the skier. The skis are edged and offer resistance to the movement. An integral part of most skiing turns.
	Distinct from side-slipping which is a technique used for losing height on a steep or awkward slope. The ski edges are released and grip is reduced enabling *gravity* to pull the skis sideways.
	Differentiated from sliding which properly refers to the skis moving along their own length, without sideways movement. This may be due to the influence of momentum, gravity or most usually, both.
Snowplough	Basic skiing posture where the skis are held in a 'V' position, tips close together, and they skid against their inner edges.
	There are two forms of snowplough: The *breaking* plough and the *gliding* plough. The breaking plough is a wide-angled posture with weighted heels, used for slowing down. The gliding plough is a narrow 'V' shape with minimum breaking effect, used to steer with and it forms part of the basic swing turn. (The weight is carred on the *whole* of the feet.)
Stem	Often used synonymously with *Snowplough*, but more correctly it describes the action of moving one ski from a parallel position to an angled position.

Style	Style is determined by the technique being performed and the skier's ability to perform it. It is the mark of his individuality, and is largely determined by the skier's physique.
Swing *(as in Swing Turn)*	A change of direction made with the skis parallel and skidding sideways. The parallel swing has the skis parallel throughout the turn, whereas the basic swing turn has the skis skidding parallel for only the latter part of the turn.
T-Bar	A ski tow which carries skiers in pairs, pulling them uphill along the surface of the snow. These lifts are also called *anchor lifts* because of the T- or anchor-shaped bar against which the skiers stand. Variations of this lift are called *button lifts* or *Poma lifts*.
Teaching Method	The means employed by an instructor to help his students to improve their skiing ability. Present ski school methods are recognized by the techniques taught to initiate basic movements, and by the order in which the basic movements are taught.
Technique	A series or 'pattern of movements' which is technically sound for a particular skill, and which is an integral part, but not the whole, of the skill. (*Barbara Knapp*.)
Toe Iron	The part of the ski binding (see *Release Bindings*) which holds the toe of the ski boot in place.
Traverse	To ski across a hill at an angle to the fall line.
Unweighting	Moving the body in relation to the skis in order to effect a reduction of weight between the skis and the snow. Unweighting can be performed by various techniques, but in most cases its purpose is to facilitate edge changing at the beginning of a turn.
Wedeln	Of German origin, *godille* in French; the term refers to continuous rhythmical linked turns close to the fall line. The British Association of Ski Instructors further defines *Wedeln* as 'having no appreciable edge set'. Rhythmical, linked turns with appreciable edge set, i.e. 'checked swings', are called *short swings*.

References

The number in parentheses immediately following the title indicates the chapter to which the reference applies.

Acquiring Ball Skills (5). H. T. A. Whiting. Bell, London, 1969

Applied Motion Study (5). F. B. and L. M. Gilbraith. Macmillan, New York, 1919

Basic Teaching System (5). British Association of Ski Instructors, Aviemore, 1979

Circuit Training (2). R. E. Morgan and G. T. Adamson. Bell, London, 1957.

Congress Report, 8th Interski, Aspen (1). Interski, Denver, 1968

Educational Psychology (5). E. Stones. Methuen, London, 1966

Examination Policy and Syllabus for the Qualification of Artificial Ski Slope Instructors (5). National Ski Federation of Great Britain. London, 1971

First Aid (5). British Red Cross Society. London, 1956

Get Fit (The Champions' Way) (2). Brian Corrigan MD and Alan Morton. Souvenir Press, London, 1968

How to Ski the New French Way (1, 3). Georges Joubert and Jean Vuarnet. Kaye and Ward, London, 1967

Inner Skiing (5). Timothy Gallwey and Bob Kriegel. Random House, New York, 1977

Introduction to Thomas Aquinas (5). Joseph Pieper. Faber and Faber, 1963

The New Official Austrian Ski System (1). Austrian Professional Ski Teachers Association. Nicholas Kaye, London, 1959

Principles of Training (2, 5). D. R. Holding. Pergamon Press, London, 1965

The Official American Ski Technique (1, 3). PSIA. Cowles Book Co., Salt Lake City, 1964

Osterreichichen Schilehrplan (1). Osterreichichen Berufschilehrer Verband. Otto Muler, Salzburg, 1972

The Science of Skiing (3). Rudi Prochazka. John Jones Cardiff, Cardiff, 1971

Ski. Vol. 35, No. 4 (1). UPD, New York, 1970

Ski, GLM (1). Morten Lund. Dial Press, New York, 1971

Ski Running (1). Crichton Sommerville, W. R. Rickmers and E. C. Richardson. Horace Cox, London, 1905

Skiing, Vol. 24, No. 2 (1). Ziff Davis, New York, 1971

Skiing Turns (1). Vivian Caulfield. Nisbett, London, 1922

Skill Analysis (3). Singer and Ramsden. McGraw-Hill, London, 1969

Skill in Sport (3, 5). Barbara Knapp. Routledge and Kegan Paul, London, 1963

The Story of Skiing (1). Arnold Lunn. Eyre and Spottiswoode, London, 1952

Strength Training for Athletics (2). Ron Pickering. Amateur Athletic Association, London, 1965

Yoga (2). Russell Atkinson. Corgi Books, London, 1967